CAROLYN GOSSAGE

GENTLEMAN SPY

THE EXPLOiTS OF FRENCH RESISTANCE HERO
ROBERT DE LA ROCHEFOUCAULD

STONE TOWER BOOKS

NEWPORT, RI

Also by Carolyn Gossage

A Question of Privilege: Canada's Independent Schools.

A History of the Frankfurt Book Fair (Translation from German)

Auf Irrfahrt—Sieben Kanadische Frauen
Unterwegs im Dritten Reich

Basilicas of Ethiopia—An Architectural History

Double Duty: Sketches and Diaries of Molly Lamb Bobak:
Canadian War Artist

Ethiopian Crosses

Ethiopian Icons

Forgotten Graces: The Travel Sketchbooks
of a Victorian Gentlewoman

Greatcoats and Glamour Boots—Canadian Women
in Uniform 1939-45 (revised edition)

Portare le Icone / Portable Icons—Art and Piety in Christian Ethiopia

Props on Her Sleeve—The Wartime Letters of a Canadian Airwoman

The Accidental Captives—The Story of Seven Women
Alone in Nazi Germany.

GENTLEMAN SPY
The Exploits of French Resistance Hero
Robert de La Rochefoucauld
Copyright © 2017 Carolyn Gossage
All rights reserved.

Stone Tower Books
Lampion Press, LLC
P. O. Box 932
Silverton, OR 97381

ISBN: 978-1-942614-28-9

Library of Congress Control Number: 2017942006

Front cover illustration by Alice Marwick
Text formatting by Amy Cole, JPL Design Solutions

Printed in the United States of America

To the memory of
Count Robert Jean-Marie De La Rochefoucauld
1923–2012

And to all who sacrificed their lives
in the name of Freedom.

"One cannot answer for his courage
when he has never been in danger."

François De La Rochefoucauld, *Maxims* (1665)

* * *

"We did not ask why; we only knew
that this was what we must do…."

Philippe de Vomécourt—*Who Lived to See the Day:
France in Arms 1940-45*

TABLE OF CONTENTS

PROLOGUE

As is so often the case, a book sometimes owes its origins to pure and simple serendipity. For me, it all began on a warm summer's morning four years ago. Having completed the wake-me-up ritual of a mug of coffee and (dare I say it ?) a cigarette, it was time to peruse the pages of Canada's venerable national paper, the Globe & Mail, for news of fresh disasters including, of course, the back page of the Sports section where the daily obituary of a deceased notable appears without fail. But the headline for today's offering dated July the 8th, 2012 captured my attention within the blink of an eye:

"ROBERT DE LA ROCHEFOUCAULD—
SECRET AGENT, 88.
A thorn in the Nazi's side and the stuff of legend"

Now here, it seemed, was a life well and truly lived! And, as I was soon to discover, this particular Second World War hero's devil-may-care flair for evading the enemy had all the earmarks of an Ian Fleming "Commander James Bond" epic adventure.

Certainly a copy of De La Rochefoucauld's Second World War memoir published in Paris should make for interesting reading, so why not follow up on my initial reaction and arrange for one to be sent to me? An accommodating British contact was equally intrigued

3

when I forwarded a copy of the original obituary, and within six weeks I was the delighted recipient of Robert De La Rochefoucauld's 2002 memoir. Even reading the summary on the back of the cover was enough to convince me that I had come upon the makings of something quite extraordinary. It was time to read on. And what a tangled tale emerged!

As recorded in his memoir—written more than fifty years after the fact—on several occasions, Robert De La Rochefoucauld was taken prisoner by the Nazis and at one stage even escaped his own execution.

Having received intensive sabotage and commando training in Britain, De La Rochefoucauld cites the fact that he was twice parachuted into Occupied France using false papers and the pseudonym René Lallier. On one mission, he writes of shooting a German guard, availing himself of the guard's uniform and making his escape—dispensing with two more German soldiers in the process.

Ever resourceful, he also made use of a highly unusual arsenal of objects in the interests of sabotage and escape, including baguettes, a stolen Nazi limousine, the leg of a table, a bicycle and a nun's habit, not to mention the more established accoutrements of espionage such as parachutes, explosives and a submarine. In short, these remarkable stories of De La Rochefoucauld's wartime feats of derring-do made for fascinating reading and appeared to prove, once again, the truth of the old chestnut that fact is often stranger than fiction. Perhaps... but then again, perhaps not!

Not long after the completion and editing of my manuscript based on intensive research and the contents of De La Rochefoucauld's personal account, it was drawn to my attention by a certain British Special Operations historian that there appeared to be a number of discrepancies in the events recorded in the erstwhile agent's memoirs. As well, according to this particular source, there was a marked absence of De La Rochefoucauld's name or pseudonym in the existing archival records of the Special

Operations Executive. Effectively, in my informant's view, the memoir was little more than the product of imaginative fabrication. A disheartening development, to say the least!

On further investigation, I was, however, encouraged to discover that these touted archival SOE records are , in fact, far from complete; partly due to attrition over the past seventy years, but also as the result of a disastrous publicly undisclosed post-war fire in which an extensive number of files went up in smoke. In addition—according to the author of the last official report of the SOE released in 1946 before it was absorbed into MI 6—the record he submitted at the time was far from exhaustive. "It is not possible," wrote Major R.A. Bourne-Patterson in his confidential report on the SOE British Circuits in France 1941—1944 compiled in 1946, "to say because an individual or circuit is not mentioned in these pages, that he or it never existed. Nor must it be assumed, because no Decoration is set against an officer's name, that he/she did not, in fact, receive one."

In the final analysis, controversy over Robert De La Rochefoucauld's memoir published almost seventy years after these dramatic feats ostensibly took place will remain a bone of contention well into the foreseeable future. Books will be written. Hollywood films may appear and their relative accuracy will undoubtedly continue to be open to question in perpetuity.

In the end, to the reader must go the spoils. Much of this memoir has an unquestionable basis in fact, but the possibility of an element of confabulation is also a reality. In the final analysis... Make of it what you will.

Carolyn Gossage
Toronto, September 2017

ACKNOWLEDGMENTS

Initially my heartfelt thanks are directed towards the members of Robert De La Rochefoucauld's immediate family: M. Jean De La Rochefoucauld, Mme. Constance Guillaumin, Mme. Hortense De La Rochefoucauld, and Mme. Astrid Gaignault. Thanks to their enthusiastic support, I was the grateful recipient of invaluable copies of vintage family photographs. The family members were also generous in the personal reassurances I received that I should feel no compunction whatever about calling upon them should I require answers to queries I might have relating to their father and his wartime memoir : *La Liberté, C'est mon plaisir*. In short, I am deeply indebted for all the time and effort expended in helping to bring the story of their remarkable father's wartime exploits to the attention of readers who may be drawn to discovering more about this little-known aspect of the War Years and the role of the Special Operations Executive (SOE).

At this juncture I also wish to extend a special thanks to La Mairie in Ouzouer-sur-Trezée which was so crucially instrumental in putting me in contact with Jean De La Rochefoucauld and " les belles soeurs".

Accolades in abundance belong to the original editor of this book, Joanna Godfrey of I. B. Tauris, London, not only for her professional expertise, but for her good cheer and ever-present support through thick and through thin. Nor do the guargantuan efforts of my dear friend, Rosmarie Epaminondas of Lima in far-away Peru go unrecognized for her inimitable copy-editing wizardry. Likewise, I offer sincerest appreciation to the Imperial War Museum's Senior Historian, Terry Charman, for his generous efforts on my behalf in terms of SOE records, medals and citations.

As well, a grateful tip of the hat to both Nancy Graham and the late Dave Broadfoot of Toronto in appreciation of their generosity in entrusting me with invaluable sources of reference from their private collections over an extended period. Merci infiniment!

Nor should I fail to mention the kindness of Professor Timothy Demy of the US Naval War College, Rhode Island for his helpful advice in terms of research resources in the UK. Additional thanks are also extended to Deborah Windsor, former Director of the Writers' Union of Canada for sharing her fascination with the amazing story of Resistance hero, Jean Moulin; to Mme Muriel Leclerc, Archivist, Musée Jean Moulin, Paris and to Madame Maryse Ghoneim, Adjointe de direction, Maison des Étudiants Canadiens, La Cité Universitaire, Paris for the warm welcome to the MEC, which served as my home base while undertaking research in April 2013.

My gratitude, as well, to m. Pierre Tillet for the use of his exhaustive record of covert British operations in France beginning in 1941 and to Richard Balesrat of the Ville de Saint-Médard-en-Jalles archives for his timely response to my queries regarding Bordeaux regional records for 1944. I would also be remiss if I neglected to profer my best wishes and good will to Paul Kix of Connecticut, whose journalistic instincts coincided with my own when he came upon the obituary of Robert De La Rochefoucauld in July 2012. In the interval—to our mutual pleasure—we have exchanged numerous e-mails and phone conversations comparing notes along the way.

And last—but far from least—to my many supportive friends and to my children, Valerie Gossage Crook of Oxford and Graeme Brookes Gossage, Toronto whose words of encouragement helped me persevere through many travails, my gratitude knows no bounds. As for my chief cook and bottle-washer (aka Carolyn's houseboy)—my photomeister and mainstay—Michael Brookes Gossage—without you, this book would never have been possible.

1 TO THE MANOR BORN

If future events are to be taken into account, it would appear that the heavenly bodies had aligned themselves most auspiciously for the birth of Robert Jean-Marie De La Rochefoucauld. At the time, of course, it would have seemed next to inconceivable that this tiny, perfect infant was destined to become a legendary hero of the Resistance in Nazi-occupied France. To those who had survived the senseless slaughter and devastation of the 1914-1918 'war to end all wars', the mere idea of France's involvement in yet another world conflict could only be described as unimaginable. Surely the terms of the Peace Accord signed in Paris in 1919 would provide the final nail in the coffin of Germany's relentless ambition for conquest?[1] Was the world not on the brink of the "Roaring Twenties" with Paris at the pulsating heart of a post-war era of fun and frivolity? Then, too, there was the need to compensate for the enormous loss of life on the battlefields.[2] Families must grow and flourish accordingly and Robert De La Rochefoucauld's aristocratic parents were no exception in as much as he was the second of what would amount to a total of ten brothers and sisters.

Robert De La Rochefoucauld's illustrious 17th-century ancestor, François VI, Duc De La Rochefoucauld, Prince de Marcillac (1613—1680) a noted author of French maxims and memoirs. Photo: www. Devoir-de-philosophie.com

In his memoirs—published in Paris in 2002—De La Rochefoucauld takes a backward glance at what appears to have been—for the most part—a blissfully carefree childhood. As part of the next generation of the French nobility, the importance of maintaining time-honoured family traditions was distinctly 'de rigeur'. Born into one of only four noble families in France whose history can be traced back a thousand years or more, the honour of those bearing the name De La Rochefoucauld was something which must be maintained in perpetuity.[3] In his memoir published in Paris in 2002, he writes:

> My family was still living, as far as possible, in the 'old ways'. My father had studied medicine, but had never practised it, although it was unquestionably a highly respectable profession and, like my mother, the daughter of the Duchess de Maillé, he was a staunch patriot. It was our mother, however, who exerted the defining influence on our education. She was a strong woman, very much at ease at 'The Hunt' yet also engaged in events of the day. She was also very much devoted

to the work of the Red Cross and served with distinction as the Chairwoman for our region.[4]

Accompanied by his siblings and assorted servants, the early years of Robert's affluent childhood were divided between the family home in Paris on the avenue de La Bourdonnais or at one or other of two idyllic chateaux—either Villeneuve close to Soissons dans l'Aisne—the ancestral home of his De La Rochefoucauld grandparents or at Châteauneuf-sur-Cher with his maternal grandmother, the Duchess of Maillé.

Among his most vivid memories of this period were the family vacations spent on board the private railway carriage belonging to his Grandmother De La Rochefoucauld, which could be readily attached onto virtually any train in order to carry everyone off in grand style to various destinations of choice throughout the length and breadth of France.

From an early age, time-honoured family traditions became an integral part of the upbringing of the young and aristocratic De La Rochefoucauld progeny. They were being 'trained up' in the style of the ancienne regime where every possible formality continued to be observed.

In his memoir, Robert De La Rochefoucauld's recollections provide a revealing glimpse into this formative stage in his life and the unforeseen implications that awaited him in the not-too-distant future.

No matter who we were staying with, one always 'dressed for dinner', and from the age of ten onwards, we were required to respect this particular custom. Moreover, we had English nannies who never allowed us to deviate from what was deemed appropriate in terms of dress and behaviour. It was also from them that I acquired an elementary grasp of English, even before I became fluent in my own language.

And it was this early knowledge of English that—quite un-expectedly—turned out to have a significant bearing on later events in the course of my life.[5]

The question of young Robert's delicate health was also brought to bear in terms of the remedy that would be selected for him by his parents in consultation with a battery of pediatric specialists. At the age of eight or nine he had spent an entire year of his once-active childhood flat on his back being rolled about on a custom-built gurney. In the light of what the future would hold in store for him within a matter of little more than a decade, it appears that the proscribed treatment for this youthful fragility proved to be miraculously effective.

Once he was sufficiently back on his feet after what must have been an extraordinarily difficult period, it was decided that Robert's educational and residual physical deficiencies would undoubtedly be improved by attendance at a series of highly reputable boys' boarding schools in the Alps, where he would purportedly benefit from the promising combination of bracing mountain air and the unquestionable erudition of his teachers. Among the institutions best remembered in his memoir—written some sixty years after the fact—was a stint in Switzerland at Villars, another at Pontoise and thereafter in Austria at a Marist Fathers' college situated not far from Salzburg.[6]

By his own admission a disruptive and undisciplined pupil, Robert appears to have blatantly demonstrated certain characteristics that failed to endear him to a succession of school administrations, with the result that, at the end of virtually every school year, Maman and Papa De La Rochefoucauld were tactfully informed that a change of schools would be in the boy's best interests. It was not that Robert was a poor student. Non, Non, Non ! In fact, quite assuredly the opposite… and hence the recommendation inevitably followed that he would best realize his full academic potential in a new and different school environment.

Family portrait taken circa 1930 featuring Madame De La Rochefoucauld with five of her ten children. Robert stands to the left of his mother. Courtesy the De La Rochefoucauld family archives.

A pair of proud young 'mariners'. Robert, on the right, outstrips his older brother, Henri, shown on the left. Courtesy the De La Rochefoucauld family archives.

Due to a childhood malady, young Robert was confined to a
flatbed for an entire year. Even the family pets at Chateau Villeneuve
seem to want to cheer up the bed-ridden young invalid. Courtesy the
De La Rochefoucauld family archives.

Robert tries his hand at Alpine skiing
after his recovery from a lengthy
convalescence at Villeneuve circa 1933.
Courtesy the De La Rochefoucauld
family archives.

What could be finer than a holiday at the seaside?
Robert (left) and his brother appear to be
enjoying every minute of it. Courtesy the De La
Rochefoucauld family archives.

Robert photographed
on the occasion of his
first communion circa
1935. Courtesy the
De La Rochefoucauld
family archives.

Family photo opportunity on the steps of Chateau Villeneuve circa 1936. Robert is seen standing behind his mother—upper right. Courtesy the De La Rochefoucauld family archives.

Pre-war photo taken to commemorate an extended family gathering at Chateau Villeneuve with assorted aunts, uncles and cousins. Robert is second from the left on the fourth step. Courtesy the De La Rochefoucauld family archives.

2

THE MAKINGS OF
A PATRIOT

During those years when the young De La Rochefoucauld's formal education still remained a work-in-progress, world affairs had taken on a disturbing and ominous turn for the worse. Beginning with the Wall Street Crash on Tuesday, October 29th, 1929, America was soon plunged into what would become a full decade of breadlines and soup kitchens as the Great Depression took its devastating toll. And in Germany, an increasingly bitter and disgruntled populace was about to embrace an ill-considered 'salvation' and begin to worship at the altar of Adolf Hitler's National Socialist Party.

By the mid 1930s, not only were the echoes of 'Sieg Heil' reverberating from the rafters of Nazi Party rallies across the length and breadth of the Fatherland but—in deliberate contravention of the terms of the Paris Peace Accord—Hitler's Germany had begun to re-arm.

The 1936 Olympic Summer Games in Berlin also provided the Nazis with a golden opportunity to promote the Führer's long entrenched policies of racial supremacy. In fact, the official Nazi party paper, the Völkischer Beobachter strongly advocated that neither Jews nor Blacks should be allowed to participate in the Games. Only when the imminent threat of a boycott by other nations was brought to bear, did the official Nazi organizers decide that an apparent change of heart would be in the best interests of furthering their ultimate agenda.

And in the midst of this increasingly threatening political scenario, during the Autumn term of 1937, while still enrolled at the Marist Fathers college near Salzburg, fifteen-year-old Robert De La Rochefoucauld found himself poised on the brink of an unforeseen and unforgettable encounter.

As a keen participant in a hale and hearty Alpine cycling expedition in the company of twenty or so of his schoolmates, De La Rochefoucauld claims to have had absolutely no prior knowledge of what lay in store. Whether by chance or by deliberate design, the group's leader had selected a route that brought the cyclists—most of them Austrians—across the border and into Southern Bavaria.

One day we rode as far as Berchtesgaden, and even proceeded upwards to the gates of Hitler's Eagle's Nest. At precisely this moment, several black cars emerged from the private driveway. The lead car came to a stop directly in front of us and who should get out, full of smiles and dressed in civilian clothes, but the Lord and Master of the Third Reich? Hitler approached the priest who was in charge of our group, asked him a few questions, as he did of my Austrian comrades, and then he turned to me. On hearing the accented German in which I attempted to address him, I was rewarded by a tap on the cheek, and the words

"Ach, so we have a young Frenchman here". [1]

Even today I wonder whether or not to admit to it, but at that moment I must confess that I was very proud indeed of this brief encounter. At the time, Adolf Hitler was vying with Joseph Stalin for recognition as the most powerful man in Europe—if not the entire world. Of course, none of us had the remotest inkling of the many atrocities already perpetrated in his name, to say nothing of the horrors which were yet to come. To be truthful—caught up as we were in our state of wide-eyed schoolboy innocence—we were all filled with admiration for this impressive leader. Here we were in the presence of the man who had given his countrymen the will to work tirelessly towards the creation of a new Germany, as well as demanding the necessary discipline that appeared to be producing impressive results.

We had also been captivated by the Swastika, as the defining symbol of Germany's Hitler Youth organizations with their emphasis on healthy outdoor activities and sports coupled with an appealing sense of camaraderie. That, at least, was our perception at the time and to a fifteen-year-old boy, it was a source of inspiration. In fact, we even went so far as to attach Swastikas onto our bicycles! [2]

Hitler's well-orchestrated plans for the future of his Third Reich had always included the adoption of the time-honoured symbol of the Swastika or Hackenkreuz as the official emblem of the emerging National Socialist Party.[3] The selection of the Swastika was Hitler's own personal choice and at the Party's Salzburg Congress held on 7 August in 1920, there appears to have been little or no opposition to his proposal. As he later noted in *Mein Kampf*:

I, myself, after innumerable attempts, had laid down a final form; a flag with a red background, a white disk, and a black swastika in the middle. After lengthy trials I also found a definite proportion between the size of the flag and the size of the white disk, as well as the shape and thickness of the swastika.[4]

In the years that followed the decision reached at the Nazi Party's Salzburg 1920 Congress to adopt Hitler's choice of the swastika as its official emblem, this ancient and mystical symbol would increasingly come to represent the very essence of oppression and evil.

Within a matter of months after his unscheduled and spontaneous interlude with the young cyclists on the road outside Bertchsgaden, the Führer gave the order for the German Wehrmacht to march across the border on 11 March 1938—the eve of a National Referendum—and, with the full co-operation of Austria's Nazi Party, to enforce the immediate annexation of Austria as a part of the Third Reich. The successful realization of the Anschluss—one of the earliest of Adolf Hitler's expansionist ambitions—was clearly the source of huge satisfaction to Party members in both countries.

By the same token, for those Austrians opposed to this well-orchestrated coup d'etat—and there were many—the repercussions that followed in the wake of this blatant act of aggression were both swift and brutal. Within a matter of weeks over 70, 000 arrests had been made, properties seized, Jews set upon and beaten and all with no apparent end in sight.[5]

The fact that the Anschluss flew in the face of the terms laid out in the 1919 Treaty of Versailles, which had unconditionally prohibited the union of the two countries, appeared to be regarded by the invading power as little more than a trifling technicality. The wheels of Nazi Germany's territorial imperative had been set in motion and they were not about to lose momentum.[6]

As an eye-witness to the Anschluss and its aftermath, virtually overnight, Robert De La Rochefoucauld's brief enthusiasm for the

Swastika was replaced by a profound and virulent revulsion against everything and everyone it represented.

> Initially, I was stupefied, but on the other hand, the Anschluss instantly opened my eyes to the duplicity and brutality of the Nazi regime and, more specifically, to that of its leader. For me, the sight of him sweeping triumphantly through the country like a conquering hero was also a kind of revelation in terms of the human capacity for inconstancy. The sight of the throngs of 'supporters' who turned out in droves to greet their new lord and master with such boundless enthusiasm was a kind of anathema. Incomprehensible, in fact! [7]

The exodus of dispossessed and disaffected Austrians, which had begun almost immediately after the Anschluss, saw the embassies of both Britain and the United States literally besieged with thousands of applications for special refugee status. Among the most notable of these Austrian émigrés was Sigmund Freud who was the last of his immediate family to seek asylum in England in the summer of 1938. Other of Freud's relatives who remained behind were less fortunate and one by one would become victims of Hitler's 'Final Solution' at the hands of the Nazis. [8]

It was a fate shared by untold numbers of Austrian Jews who had failed to make good their escape before being seized and dispatched to meet their deaths at one of the infamous Nazi Death Camps. A much-celebrated exception was the destiny of the Georg von Trapp family, whose 1938 flight from Nazi-occupied Austria was later immortalised by Richard Rodgers and Oscar Hammerstein in what would become their last collaboration: "The Sound of Music" which first appeared on Broadway in the early 1960s. [9]

Looking back to these turbulent times, Robert De La Rochefoucauld writes of his return to the family home in Paris at the end of his "Anschluss" semester in Salzburg. If previous accounts of his deportment at boarding school are any indication, it may well be that he was less than enchanted by the prospect of a return to his studies. On the other hand, his personal observations in Austria had undoubtedly made him more acutely aware of the tide of political turmoil sweeping across Europe.

In the late autumn of 1938, as a student in Paris, he would also have learned almost immediately of the fatal shooting at the German Embassy of a young German diplomat, Ernst vom Rath by a radical 17-year-old Jewish dissident. It was an act which would precipitate the infamous Kristallnacht rampage of anti-Semitic brutality at the hands of Hitler Youth and Nazi Storm Troopers that swept literally overnight throughout Germany as well as parts of recently annexed Austria.[10]

Churchill's biographer, Martin Gilbert, later wrote that no event in the history of German Jews between 1933 and 1945 was more widely reported upon at precisely the moment when it was actually occurring. The ensuing accounts of Kristallnacht from foreign journalists writing from within Germany sent instantaneous shock waves around the world.

The following day, the London *Times* commentary on the impact of these reports did not mince words. "No foreign propagandist bent upon blackening Germany before the world could outdo the tale of burnings and beatings, of blackguardly assaults on defenceless and innocent people, which disgraced that country yesterday."

Not unexpectedly, the German propaganda machine represented the entire debacle of 9 November as little more than isolated acts of vengeance by overzealous young National Socialists brought on by the cold-blooded murder of a German diplomat in Paris by a despicable Jewish assassin. No further comment was deemed necessary.

Doubtless there were more than a few intense discussions within the De La Rochefoucauld household as the events of the coming months found Europe once again teetering on the brink of disaster. Judging from the comments and observations made in his memoir, it seems abundantly clear that young Robert De La Rochefoucauld was fully aware of the political implications of Hitler's relentless campaign of aggression and the threat it posed to the future of his country:

> We could feel War approaching, and the cowardly Munich agreements did nothing to reassure us. Nor did the optimistic proclamations of the government and of General Gamelin. Or—for that matter—the empty defense of the Maginot Line, which left our border with Belgium completely exposed. Belgium's state of neutrality had been designed to ensure that it could not be invaded by German Forces. In the end, however, it was a pathetically misguided hope that proved to be nothing more than a snare and a delusion.
>
> When war with Germany was officially declared in early September 1939, I was close to celebrating my 17th birthday. We were about to enter that period commonly referred to as 'the Phoney War'.[11] The French and the Germans faced each other like hostile guard dogs without actually engaging in combat, while in the East, thanks to the Soviet-German Pact, the German Army and the Red Army took their time dismembering Poland. Having settled the fate of that unfortunate country, the German Army launched its offensive into France on 10 May 1940, through Belgium and around the Maginot Line. By 15 May, 1940, the German swastika was flying over French territory.[12]

During this lengthy eight-month period of suspended hostilities—which was, in effect, a debilitating war of nerves—the people of France had become increasingly apprehensive. To make matters worse, public opinion was sharply divided. After the devastating losses suffered as a result of the Great War of 1914–1918, many in France were reluctant to support another call to arms against what appeared to be an invincible force. On the other hand, the unquenchable flame of patriotism continued to burn brightly in the hearts of those who refused to follow the path of pacifism.

Clearly, the sympathies of the De La Rochefoucauld family most assuredly did not embrace a defeatist outlook, however several more years would pass before their second-born son, Robert, would finally be in a position to actively take part in the fight to rid France of its enemies from within and without.

The ultimate Fall of France—the result of a swift and well-orchestrated invasion by the German Wehrmacht—was the outcome of two strategic operations. In the first, German armoured units pushed through the Ardennes to cut off and surround the Allied units that had advanced into Belgium. When the combined British and French forces were relentlessly pushed back to the sea, the British launched Operation Dynamo—the legendary nine-day evacuation of the British Expeditionary Force along with several French divisions from the beaches and harbor of Dunkirk between 26 May and 4 June 1940. Prime Minister Winston Churchill hailed it as a "miracle of deliverance".[13]

Then on 5 June, Germany embarked upon the second phase of its invasion. At first, the depleted French forces put up a valiant effort to repulse the German onslaught, but gradually they were overwhelmed by German air superiority. Hitler's army pushed ever deeper into France and within ten days his troops had arrived in the heart of an undefended Paris.

In her book on the women of the French Resistance, author Caroline Moorehead provides a highly evocative description of the initial reaction to this inglorious event. She writes:

What surprised the Parisians, standing in little groups along the Champs-Elysées to watch the German soldiers take over their city in the early hours of 14 June 1940, was how youthful and healthy they all looked. Tall, fair, clean-shaven, the young men marching to the sounds of a military band to the Arc de Triomphe were observed to be wearing uniforms of good cloth and gleaming boots made of real leather. The coats of the horses pulling the cannons glowed. It seemed not an invasion but a spectacle. Paris itself was calm and almost totally silent. Other than the steady waves of tanks, motorised infantry and troops, nothing moved. And when they stopped staring, the Parisians returned to their homes and waited to see what would happen....[14]

They would not have long to wait.

France's venerable hero of The Great War, Marshal Philippe Pétain—contrary to the desires of a number of his countrymen—announced that he would seek an Armistice. On 22 June, an agreement was signed between France and Germany, which resulted in the arbitrary division of the country. Germany would occupy the north and west and in the south an unoccupied zone—the zone libre—would be governed by the newly-formed Vichy government under the dubious leadership of the aging Marshal Pétain.

A further humiliating and demoralizing clause in Pétain's capitulation also specified that the Occupying Power would be permitted to keep the roughly two million French soldiers they had captured in their military offensive as prisoners-of-war in Germany. The traditions of warfare must be satisfied.

As for the fate of the De La Rochefoucauld family in Paris:

In the wake of the German advance, we first took refuge at Châteauneuf-sur-Cher which was still in the unoccupied zone. Then, a little later, as the exodus of refugees from the Occupied Zone began clogging the roads, we retreated to the château at Villeneuve which was set on 150 hectares of beautiful, fertile farmland in the north-east. A former abbey, it had been razed by the Germans in 1914 before being rebuilt as a château in the post-war era.

As the Germans advanced onto French soil, I followed the ensuing events with an increasing sense of despair. Once the 'Phoney War' had run its course, I had pinned all my hopes on a return to the redemption of France's honour. But then came Marshal Pétain's agreement to sign an Armistice.

To say that I was opposed to it would, in fact, amount to an understatement. I was adamantly against this capitulation—as was my entire family. It was the first time I had actually seen my mother brought to tears over the fate of her beloved France. And even more distressing was the knowledge that my father had been taken prisoner and our poor mother had received no news of him other than the fact that he was being held at Stalag XVII Ain Germany.[15]

A jubilant Adolph Hitler struts though Paris in the shadow of the Eiffel Tower with other members of the Nazi High Command following the fall of France on 20 June 1940. Credit: Bundesarchiv—Militär Archiv, Freiburg.

To make matters worse, there appears to have been a preponderance of public support for the Armistice and initially, at least, the general reaction was one of relief and even gratitude to Marshal Pétain. In retrospect, from young Robert De La Rochefoucauld's personal vantage point, anyone who capitulated was nothing less than a traitor.

It seemed absolutely monstrous to me that Pétain had agreed to sign the Armistice, but de Gaulle's Free French broadcasts from London brought us a glimmer of hope. In spite of increasing difficulty because the Germans had immediately begun jamming the BBC broadcasts, we listened every day without fail. Like de Gaulle, I, too, believed that France had lost a battle, but certainly not the war. To me it seemed entirely clear that national honour demanded we must continue the fight. In fact, my friends and I spoke of little else.[16]

Given the choice, we would have loved the opportunity to join the Free French in England. But how to go about it? The incident of the Parisian students who had dared to place a bouquet on the tomb of The Unknown Soldier on 11 November 1940 gave us a glimmer of hope. Had I known of it, I would have gladly joined them. At least now we knew that our sentiments were shared by other young people who were willing to commit acts of defiance.[17]

But while the presence of the Germans was almost unbearable, any hope of being rid of them was little more than a distant dream. At this point, there could be nothing forthcoming from the Soviet Union, due in large part to Stalin's signature on a non-aggression pact with The Reich. Nor was there much more to hope for from the United States following Roosevelt's re-election and his apparent avowal that he would never be persuaded to send American boys overseas to join the fight in Europe.[18]

The presence of de Gaulle and the Free French in London was at least a reminder that the fight for freedom in France was not entirely a lost cause.

German troops march past the Arch of Triumph in Paris following the surrender of France only six weeks after the initial 'Blitzkrieg' invasion on 13 May 1940.
Credit: Bundesarchiv -Militärarchiv, Freiburg.

German signposts erected in Paris for the convenience
of the Occupying Forces. Photo by Andre Zucca for a
German propaganda magazine.

3

SAVED BY THE POSTMAN

While Robert De La Rochefoucauld and his friends dreamed of a future where they could take an active part in the fight against the Boche, others had already begun to find their own ways to be quietly obstructive. In fact, the ink was barely dry on the armistice agreement before individual French men and women opted to engage in their own independent acts of personal resistance. There was the farm worker—and veteran of the Great War—who climbed a telephone pole near a German airfield and cut the lines. This particular act of patriotism would cost him his life.[1]... the Mother Superior of the Ste. Agonie Convent in Paris, Henriette Frede, who—along with nine of her nuns—took on the dangerous mission of operating a clandestine radio transmitter in an attic above the chapel sacristy in order to communicate with London.[2]... And then there was the frail-looking old Parisian woman sitting on a stool, who kept a daily vigil at the bottom of the stairs in carefully selected Métro stations patiently waiting for the opportunity to trip up German officers with a deftly placed walking stick... followed, of course, by an apologetic

33

"Oh, pardon, monsieur!" as her victim dusted himself off, recovered his lost dignity and went on his way. She evidently kept a daily tally and was sorely disappointed if her average was not somewhere between thirty and forty pratfalls.[3]

View of the Chateaux de Villeneuve near Soissons
by late-18th century artist, Tavernier de Jonquières.
Photo courtesy of La Bibliothèque Nationale.

Far from Paris, sequestered in the relative safely of the family chateau in the countryside, young Robert De La Rochefoucauld made no secret of his Gaullist sympathies and his disdain for those in the defeatist camp. Among family and friends this 'loose talk' posed no particular threat, however—even in this relatively rural setting—it was not long before word of this spread beyond the confines of those who shared his views and reached the ears of someone with distinctly malicious intent. When it came to discretion, experience would become the best teacher. He recounted:

I did have trouble coming to terms with sitting idly by as the people of France endured the combined wretchedness of the Occupation and the privations of food rationing during 1940 and 1941. In fact, I found myself increasingly obsessed with the idea of somehow finding a way to escape from France and join General de Gaulle and his Free French forces in London.

It goes almost without saying that my mother was equally incensed about the dire conditions imposed on those living under the forces of Occupation and well understood my restlessness. In any event, one morning a certain postal employee from nearby Soissons called discreetly at the chateau asking specifically to speak with my mother. It seems that our visitor was the person charged with the task of sorting the local mail and he explained that he had come upon quite a number of letters addressed to the Gestapo in the course of performing his duties.

Whenever he found one, he set it aside to take home with him and proceeded to place the envelope over a steaming kettle. In cases where he found a denunciation—which sadly was more frequently than it should have been—if he knew the person or person who had been named, he made it his business to warn them before destroying the letter in question. At that point, he handed my mother an anonymous letter in which I was denounced as a dangerous anti-German terrorist and a Gaullist into the bargain.

It is next to impossible to express the enormous gratitude we felt towards this courageous man, working alone, not a member of any network—a man with nothing to gain— who was taking huge risks in order to save me as well as countless others from falling into enemy hands. Although this was our first and last meeting, I have always deeply regretted never having had the occasion to set eyes on this man again, for not long afterwards, he disappeared into the unknown. And without the knowledge that his intercession had shaped my destiny.

This incident occurred at the beginning of 1942. We quickly understood that after this denunciation—so fortunately intercepted—others would not fail to follow and might achieve their intended purpose. There were unquestionably more than a few who might want to contribute to my downfall by denouncing me: collaborators certainly, and also any number of Communists who had been infuriated by the fact that we Gaullists had never negotiated with or supported them— either before the War or at the time when, by reason of party discipline, they could have aligned themselves with Germany by virtue of the German-Soviet Pact. I was, therefore, in considerable danger and would have to leave. This was, for me, the beginning of a great adventure into the unknown.[4]

The provocation of De La Rochefoucauld's indiscriminate diatribes clearly dictated an escape from the imminent denunciation and arrest awaiting him in Soissons. But without any specific contact with the organized Resistance, his options were painfully limited.

I knew scarcely anything of the activities of the Resistance except what I had gleaned from cryptic messages broadcast from London or by the local "news" which was distorted if not totally fabricated and under the rigorous control of the German propaganda sources or the Vichy government.[5]

The best solution appeared to be a return to Paris where he could take advantage of a greater degree of anonymity. By hiding in plain sight on the city's crowded streets and smoke-filled cafes, De La Rochefoucauld's chances of being denounced were substantially reduced, however, there remained the problem of finding a trustworthy contact within the Resistance. Someone who would be in a position to provide him with the solution to his dilemma. It would be a risky business.

By the Spring of 1942, the Gestapo in Paris were working overtime to hunt down every possible suspect who might lead them to uncover a link to the Resistance. After two grim years of life under the heel of German authority—marked by the darkness of the curfews, restrictions on movement, and crippling shortages of every description—the anti-Nazi sentiments of many Parisians had become firmly entrenched, but the spectre of betrayal, arrest and interrogation remained a deterrent to all but the most courageous.

Eventually I ran into a fellow in Paris whom I knew slightly and had reason to believe was a supporter of the Resistance. After a few conversations, I decided to risk confessing to him my desire to get to London and join de Gaulle. This confession, in the climate of that particular time, was—at the very least—another of my youthful indiscretions: but in this case, it proved to be one that worked out to my distinct advantage.

Although regrettably he was not in a position to help me directly, he assured me that one of his trusted friends worked for governmental services in the Vichy sector and had already provided assistance to several potential Free French volunteers and helped them make their way to England. Obviously it would be useful for me to be in touch with this friend. What's more, he declared himself willing to arrange a meeting for me with his contact at the earliest possible opportunity. Needless to say, I was more than delighted to accept this generous offer.[6]

In the end, it had all been well worth the risk. The two agreed to meet again in a week's time and in the interval, the provision of false identity cards, papers and other necessities would be arranged for. In a burst of enthusiasm, De La Rochefoucauld divulged to his new-found friend that he had already concocted a nom de guerre for himself. He would be René Lallier, a pseudonym he had picked out of the air, but which had the distinct advantage of preserving his own initials.

At their next meeting, the same nameless friend confirmed that he had succeeded in setting up a rendez-vous with his contact in the Unoccupied Zone to the south. Within a few days, Monsieur René Lallier was expected to check in at a certain hotel in Vichy—then the provisional capital of France—and wait for someone to contact him.

Scarcely believing his good luck, De La Rochefoucauld purchased a train ticket and was soon en route to the city of Vichy where Pétain and his adherents held sway. As a complete stranger here, he was understandably suspicious of everything and everyone and took pains to be as unobtrusive as possible as he made his way to the designated hotel. After booking a room, he settled in to wait for word from his contact. So far, so good.

The day after his arrival, he was informed by the front desk that 'monsieur' had a visitor. But was this the person he had been pinning his hopes on? His first contact on the road to a safe passage to London? Only time would tell.

Initially, the caller took the sensible precaution of engaging in banal conversation in order to observe and assess the young man who had purportedly been sent to him in good faith. It was imperative that he be absolutely certain this was not an imposter attempting to infiltrate the escape route. The nightmare of betrayal was never far removed, and—all in good time—Robert De La Rochefoucauld would experience for himself the realization of this ever-present fear.

Having finally laid all his suspicions to rest, De La Rochefoucauld's contact gave him instructions for the next stop on his itinerary. He was to proceed further south to Perpignan where arrangements were in place for him to meet yet another 'friend'.[7] In turn, this man would put him in touch with a group belonging to the local Resistance. The principal function of these members of the so-called 'Army of Shadows' was to provide assistance to those in need of being spirited across the French border and into Spain.[8]

De La Rochefoucauld was then given the name and address of their man in Perpignan and instructed to memorize the information. Above all, he must never—under any circumstances—yield to the temptation to write anything down. This was a proven precaution that could well make all the difference between life and death.

Slowly but surely, De La Rochefoucauld was being introduced to the essential rules of conduct so necessary in the fugitive life he was about to embrace.

So at the beginning of the summer of 1942, I set out for Perpignan, having placed in my wallet a new identity card in the name of René Lallier. At the address I had been given and duly memorised, I met a man of about thirty, who had been informed in advance of my impending visit. He was immediately gracious and welcomed me as warmly as if we had been friends forever. It turned out that he was ostensibly working in Perpignan as a bureaucrat. At least this was his 'cover' while engaging in more patriotic undertakings on the side and I felt enormously grateful to him when he offered to put me up while I waited for my passage to Spain.

And—as things turned out—my host's offer proved to be immensely fortunate for me because as a virtual fugitive I had to wait there for almost two weeks. Finally, the word came through that the Resistance group I had been told about was in the process of making arrangements for two British airmen to cross the mountains into Spain and—best of all—I would be included as part of the same operation. At least now, the reason for the long delay had become clear.

On the appointed day, my host and I had to board a wheezing old bus, powered by a gargantuan generator, which took us laboriously up winding mountain roads to a small village about twenty kilometres from Perpignan. Here we were to wait for the arrival of the Resistance group's contact. Before long the fellow turned up and it was then time for me to bid a final farewell to my Perpignan host and helpful new friend. Then, accompanied by my new 'mentor', the two of us started off on foot to reach the Resistance group's camp which lay just a few kilometres ahead.

In the depths of a dense mountain forest, we joined a group of about ten men, all very amiable, whose appearance fit identically with my boyhood image of bold adventurers. In any case, they certainly bore a greater resemblance to smugglers than to members of the Salvation Army—and indeed with good reason! My companion explained to me that these fellows knew the border area better than anyone else because they had spent years upon years engaged in the cross-border smuggling of cigarettes and alcohol. He did add, however, that they had long since honourably dedicated themselves to the safe passage of downed aviators and agents of the French Underground.[9]

The following day the long-awaited British aviators finally arrived in camp. Nor did it come as any great surprise that neither of them spoke a word of French. On the other hand, this linguistic shortfall presented De La Rochefoucauld with an opportunity to test out his skills as a translator—and quite successfully as it turned out. The two were seasoned Royal Air Force (RAF) men—one a pilot and the second a radio operator, and both appeared substantially older than their nineteen-year-old interpreter.

They had evidently been shot down on a mission over Nazi-occupied France, but had luckily been able to deploy their parachutes and elude German patrols before making contact with the right people. They had then set out on the long and furtive route that would eventually lead them out of harm's way as they were passed along from one safe house or hiding place to another. As they moved in succession from one link in the chain of escape to the next, they were fed, clothed and provided with shelter… and all at enormous personal risk to those willing to assist them.

4 ACROSS THE BORDER TO SPAIN

Now at last they were on freedom's threshold. It was decided that, despite the inherent risks of climbing through the mountains in the pitch dark, the party would leave for Spain the following evening. Because of the frequency of patrols on either side of the border, this was a journey that could best be attempted under cover of darkness. When they set out, there were seven in the group—four local guides known as *passeurs*, the two British airmen, and one young Frenchman, Robert De La Rochefoucauld. The climb proved to be a difficult one as the group wended its tortuous way in single-file along steep trails known only to the local inhabitants—with a scout always moving a good distance ahead of the rest of the party.

Every two hours they would take a much-needed break for a quarter of an hour before moving ever onwards and upwards until they reached the point where they were almost at the border. By now, the darkness had faded into dawn and they were forced to spend the remains of the day in hiding, counting the hours and waiting anxiously for the signal that it was safe to proceed.

We started off again in the dead of night. Our trek continued to be difficult, but it was also becoming more and more dangerous: many times we almost ran into patrols of French border officials accompanied by German militia. Finally, near Le Perthus Pass, we crossed the border into Spain and it was here that our four escorts left us to return to their camp and await the next group in need of their invaluable assistance.[1]

As for my companions and myself; we found ourselves almost delirious with joy and relief as we savoured our first taste of freedom. We had actually made the crossing without incident and this in itself was certainly cause for celebration. But in spite of our shared optimism, our situation was still more than a little uncertain since we were at a complete loss about how to proceed in a region that was totally unfamiliar to any of us. Our one consolation was that at least we had a plan. Not only that, but it was a plan that appeared perfectly straightforward and sensible. We would simply make our way to the nearest city, take a train from there to Madrid, and immediately present ourselves at the British Embassy.

We stepped out briskly and in the best of spirits until around 10 o'clock that morning when we reached the outskirts of a fairly large town. We were foolish enough to assume that this was a good sign, but it turned out that our optimism was sadly misplaced. Within minutes of our approach, we ran straight into a Spanish Border Patrol which took one look at us and decided our appearance was distinctly suspicious: three bedraggled looking men who bore a greater resemblance to highway men than law-abiding citizens.

Given the circumstances, to me it only made sense to reveal the truth of our situation to the one member of the patrol who spoke French: "I have just escaped from France and my companions are two Royal Air Force officers shot down by the Germans." This information obviously came as no great surprise to our captors and although the Spaniards did show a certain respect towards the British officers, the subaltern explained to us that he was nonetheless obliged to arrest us.

In almost the blink of an eye, we had gone from freedom to captivity. And, I might add, not the least bit enraptured by this turn of events. We were soon passed on from one authority to the next and each time were required to repeat our story and respond to the questions posed by assorted Spanish bureaucrats. We'd come directly out of the frying pan into the fire.[2]

The forbidding exterior of General Franco's Miranda Prison just south of the French-Spanish border where De La Rochefoucauld and two British airmen spent miserable two months in 1942.
Photo credit: Archivo General Militar, Spain.

In due course, the gates of the infamous Miranda pris-
on-cum-concentration camp closed on the three benighted captives
and they were escorted to the section of the camp reserved for foreign political prisoners. Here the three detainees were allotted a cell,
however, despite their insistent protests, there was absolutely no information forthcoming with regard to the length of their stay in this
unsavoury place.[3]

With the three of them confined to a single cell, there was precious little elbow room and these cramped quarters combined with
insufficient or inedible food only heightened their heartfelt desire to
be released from this unforeseen incarceration at the earliest possible moment. And yet, without realizing it at the time, this enforced
period of confinement proved to be extremely useful when it came
to the future role in store for a certain young Frenchman whose head
remained filled with dreams of service to his country.[4]

To begin with, the situation offered him the opportunity to im-
prove his command of spoken English immeasurably, as he and his
fellow prisoners swopped stories to help keep up their spirits as they
endured what must have been a mutually frustrating predicament.
Within weeks, the three had forged a firm bond of friendship that
precluded national differences and for De La Rochefoucauld this
proximity also provided him with an insight into what it meant to
be an Englishman. This was a facet of their shared ordeal at Miranda
that proved to be an unforeseen and unimagined advantage—an advantage which, in the fullness of time, would serve him well on more
than one occasion.

With just cause, the two airmen were instantly consumed by
their desire to contact the British Embassy in Madrid and, in fact,
not a single day of their captivity passed without an urgent request
for their release being submitted either verbally or in writing. For
De La Rochefoucauld, on the other hand, the only recourse would
have been to establish communication with the French Ambassador,

who, as a representative of the Vichy government in Spain, would have proven to be anything but helpful. Clearly the only hope for release would be a request on his behalf through the good offices of his British cellmates.

After two long months of what must have felt closer to a virtual eternity, the two RAF officers were escorted to a meeting room where they could finally confer with a representative of their Embassy who had driven to Miranda from Madrid for this express purpose. Nor did they neglect to mention to the man from Madrid the plight of their French comrade and strongly recommend his intercession, explaining that De La Rochefoucauld's only desire was to get to London, meet with General de Gaulle and offer his services. After about half an hour, the two returned to their cell wreathed in smiles. M. De La Rochefoucauld had been requested to present himself immediately to the Embassy representative. This was certainly unexpected:

Somewhat flabbergasted, I found myself in the presence of a British Officer who looked to be a man of about 35 or so. He introduced himself as Major Picquet-Wicks, and began by thanking me profusely for what I had done to help his compatriots. Since circumstances had really not allowed me to do very much—other than serving as their translator—I realised that my RAF friends had substantially embellished my role in their escape through the mountains. The major listened attentively as I did my utmost to assure him that I had made my way from Occupied France into Spain with one specific objective in mind—the possibility of somehow getting to London and joining the forces of General de Gaulle and the Free French.

After having given some thought to my impassioned declaration of purpose, he promised he would do everything in his power to ensure that I could, indeed, embark for London at the same time as the two officers of the Royal Air Force. Thanking him effusively, I hurried back to our cell to enthusiastically embrace my new friends who had so adeptly advanced my chances of realising my distant dream. After all that we three had endured together, it was a moment of shared euphoria. The day was at hand when we would be turning our backs on the filth of Miranda and its enforced degradation. And from our standpoint, that day could not arrive soon enough!

Within a week, we were informed that we had been official-ly liberated. What's more, there was a car and driver from the Embassy of Great Britain ready and waiting for us at the main entrance of Miranda Prison. Within a matter of minutes, we three jubilant inmates found ourselves rolling happily down the road leading to Madrid. It was high time for a celebration!

Night had already fallen when we arrived in the Spanish capital and the city was brilliantly illuminated. And what a beautiful sight it was for us—grown all too accustomed to the inky blackness imposed by the wartime restrictions in both Paris and in London! After those months and years of living in the dark, we had all but forgotten what it was like to experience the warm glow of city lights.

Once delivered to the Embassy, we were given a hearty wel-come by our 'guardian angel'—the efficient and charming Major Eric Picquet-Wicks—to whom I expressed my pro-found gratitude for the exceptional assistance he had afford-ed me.[5] Since the Ambassador himself was absent at that time, it was not until the following morning that we could be introduced to him. In the meantime, we were presented with an excellent dinner and then escorted to our accommodations, whose size and comfort struck us as next to inconceivable after our two-month stint behind the bars of a prison cell. The following morning, the luxury and abundance of a real English breakfast left us on the verge of disbelief. Our deliverance had indeed been the closest imaginable thing to an overnight miracle.

Shortly thereafter we were ushered in to meet the Ambassador, Samuel Hoare, and it was at that moment that my destiny took on a slightly different complexion.[6] A charming gentleman, who spoke impeccable French, this distinguished representative of His Britannic Majesty thanked me profusely for the assistance I was alleged to have provided to his compatriots. At the same time he made it clear to me that he knew of my ambition to join the forces of the Free French in London. On the other hand, with the utmost tact, he indicated that I might not be aware that there were other possibilities open to me, should I be interested.

Eric Piquet-Wicks who brought Jean Moulin to No. 1 Dorset Square

Major Eric Piquet-Wicks, the man responsible for recruiting Robert De La Rochefoucauld for the SOE after arranging his release from confinement at Miranda Prison. Photo credit: Jarrolds Press, London.

Without in any way undermining the well-intentioned worth of my original goal, he then proposed an alternative plan. What would I say to the idea of being enlisted into the British Special Operations Executive which was in the process of carrying out wartime missions in France?

Ambassador Hoare then went on to explain to me the reasons behind this rather unusual proposition. He pointed out that British-born agents had a level of competence and courage that was beyond reproach and they had also expended a great deal of time and effort in achieving a high degree of competence in the French language. However, despite their best efforts, many of these agents were unable to overcome the inherent difficulties of French pronunciation. In fact, in some cases their accents were nothing short of appalling!

At this point, I had to stop and think. Was this really the British Ambassador making such an observation, or had I simply imagined it? Much later I would have just cause to admit that his remarks were not without justification for—on occasion—the questionable French accents of certain British agents were what gave them away. And once in enemy hands, their fate was effectively sealed.

With great candour, Ambassador Hoare went on explain that it was no simple matter for would-be agents to be taken on as SOE operatives: They would be required to undergo a period of intensive and highly rigorous training and this alone was extremely difficult. It did, however, provide those charged with the all-important task of evaluating the trainees with the opportunity to scrutinise and assess the physical and mental aptitude of each candidate.

Then came Ambassador Hoare's final query: "How old are you, my boy?". How should I answer? With the truth or a reply that—under the circumstances would be more acceptable? I chose to lie.

"Twenty-one," came my immediate response knowing full well that I had added two years to my actual age. We were then at the end of the month of November 1942 and I had celebrated—if I could call it that—my nineteenth birthday in September of that year.[7]

As the interview drew to its conclusion, De La Rochefoucauld extended his utmost gratitude to the Ambassador for making this unexpected proposal and left him in no doubt that he was fully aware of the honour just conferred on him Still, he was determined to remain true to his original ambition to meet with General de Gaulle. In the event that he received the General's authorization to serve with the British Special Forces, he would then proceed accordingly. Ambassador Hoare gave every assurance that he completely understood this position and went on to discuss the various options available for getting him off to England with dispatch.

Evidently there were two possibilities open to him. The first would be to make the journey by boarding a submarine in Gibraltar and the second option was a flight which would take him directly from Madrid to London. This was obviously a more expedient alternative, but not necessarily without its own unforeseen complications.

As luck would have it, the Ambassador himself had just been called to London, so the choice had effectively been made. When the time came, Robert De La Rochefoucauld and the two RAF boys would accompany his Excellency on the flight to Mother England.

5

LONDON AT LAST

A week later, the assembled passengers, including Ambassador Hoare, Major Picquet-Wicks, the two British aviators and De La Rochefoucauld took their seats on board a B-17 Flying Fortress and winged their way safely over the Atlantic, following a course that kept them a healthy distance away from the coast of France. Within a few short hours, they were in British air space and making the final approach for a landing at a military base somewhere in the vicinity of Birmingham.

To celebrate their arrival in England's green and pleasant land, the base commander offered his visitors a hearty welcome and suggested that a drink to toast their safe return would be in order. All too soon, though, it was time for everyone to go their separate ways… a time for exchanging farewells. Farewell to Ambassador Hoare, who had shown his guests such warm hospitality, but also farewell to Robert De La Rochefoucauld's companions in captivity— the two British airmen whose names remain unknown but whose friendship was remembered for a lifetime. Each took their leave full of promises to meet again, but like so many wartime promises, this was one which would never be kept. Within the next few months, De

La Rochefoucauld learned with deep regret that his friends had both been killed in action.[1]

My farewells were scarcely over when I was crammed into a Military Police vehicle which took me to a camp somewhere just outside London. Major Picquet-Wicks accompanied me and explained that my stay here was part of a procedure whereby newcomers were placed under observation for a given period. On arrival, he introduced me to the camp commander to whom he gave a detailed explanation of my situation. In addition, he emphasized the fact that I was a volunteer, or—at the very least—someone amenable to the possibility of being enlisted into the British Special Operations Executive. Before leaving, he also passed on to me the information I must retain, should the need arise for getting in touch with him. And for the moment, that was it. I was on my own.

Once in the camp, which was apparently a former barracks—I found myself in the company of about twenty other 'illegals'—referring, I suppose, to the fact that they, too, had arrived in England from various European countries by irregular means: Poles, Belgians, two or three Frenchmen and one from Luxembourg. It turned out that each of us had his own story about how he had managed to arrive in England— and often under the most improbable circumstances.

One fellow described how he had made it across the Channel in a small sailing vessel. Another—and perhaps the most daring account of all—was the story told by a chap who had 'borrowed' a light aircraft from an airfield somewhere in German-occupied territory and actually succeeded in landing it on British soil. I also discovered that—like my-self—quite a number of my companions had arrived in our midst by means of a similarly risky escape route through the mountains and into Spain.

Today it is no secret that, for the English, the main purpose behind this imposed quarantine was to establish with certainty that none of us were enemy infiltrators. The camp was, in effect, a sort of screening facility where new arrivals could be put through an intensive series of interrogations in order to establish their credibility—or lack of it.

As for myself, I was questioned by both the English and the French. Fortunately for me, one of the Frenchmen present knew certain members of my family, and I was therefore in a position to speak about them in detail. This was taken as al-most indisputable proof of the authenticity of my statements and, as a result, my quarantine was reduced to a bare mini-mum. Within a week after my arrival at the camp, with my identity fully validated, I was informed that I was free to leave[2]

First and foremost on De La Rochefoucauld's agenda was the question of making contact with the Staff Headquarters of the Free French in order to present himself and outline the proposition made to him by Ambassador Hoare in Madrid. If all went according to plan, De La Rochefoucauld would then obtain authorization to enlist in the British Special Operations Executive or SOE—the clandestine organization set up in July 1940 at the instigation of Prime Minister Churchill. Its primary objective was to wreak as much havoc as possible in Nazi-occupied Europe by supplying the much-needed arms and personnel required to help conduct an effective undercover campaign of sabotage and general disruption.[3]

Sir Winston Churchill, sporting a submachine gun.
The Prime Minister was the moving force behind
the establishment of the SOE and guerrilla warfare
in Nazi-occupied Europe in 1940.
Photo credit: Churchill Archives, Cambridge.

The new arrival in England would undoubtedly have been provided with some sort of presentable clothing—perhaps even a suit—
before leaving the camp where he had spent a week in the precautionary ' holding tank '. Someone must also have provided him with
sufficient pocket money to see him through for a reasonable amount
of time.

Adhering to his own well-formulated strategy, Robert De La
Rochefoucauld had long-since decided that his best chance for success
was to go directly to the top with no stops along the way. He would
proceed to the Free French headquarters at Carlton Gardens near The
Mall and request a meeting with General de Gaulle in person.

At this juncture General Charles de Gaulle had been in London for nearly two and a half years. On 11 November 1942, the Germans had invaded the Free Zone formerly under the control of Petain's Vichy government with the result that the entire country was now in the hands of its Nazi oppressors. Surely this would encourage more French citizens to rally to the cause of the Resistance.

Having been successfully extricated from France in June of 1940 with scarcely a moment to spare, de Gaulle had been welcomed by Prime Minister Churchill and offered temporary quarters until the premises at Carlton Gardens could be made available for use as his Headquarters. It was from here on 18 June that he had made the first of his regular broadcasts transmitted by the BBC to the people of France in the hope of inspiring them to set aside all thoughts of defeatism and to rally to the cause of freedom.[4]

A British driver obligingly dropped me off at the Free French Headquarters at its prestigious Carlton Gardens address and after making initial contact with a Staff Officer, I was introduced to the General de Gaulle's aide-de-camp, Geoffroy de Courcel, who received me most amiably. Possibly a certain familiarity with the De La Rochefoucauld name helped facilitate matters, but there was no indication of this at the time. I explained my situation to him and expressed my earnest desire to meet with the General personally.

As luck would have it, de Gaulle happened to be in his office at precisely that moment and de Courcel informed me that it would be his pleasure to make the introduction. The Great Man himself would then consider my proposal and provide me with his decision. You can well imagine my reaction to the prospect of being introduced on the spot to the legendary General Charles de Gaulle, whose distant voice—made even more surreal by the static interference that the Germans generated on the BBC's London broadcasts—had inspired me from afar. This was the man who represented for me—and for so many others—the very soul of France and the pursuit of its freedom! [5]

After extending a cordial greeting, the General began by extending his gratitude to me for my earlier aspirations to enlist in the Forces of Free France. I then proceeded to explain my dilemma—the fact that I had also received a proposal from the British, who had suggested that they would welcome my enlistment in their covert service and—more specifically—my participation in clandestine missions within France. [6]

De La Rochefoucauld went on to explain to the General that one of the primary reasons behind this offer by the British was the knowledge that some of the covert agents involved in missions into France had failed to overcome the inherent difficulties of pronunciation. By their own admission, this inadequacy with the spoken language had put British operations in France at a distinct disadvantage, to the degree that the unmistakeably Anglophone accents of certain agents had rendered them more readily identifiable and therefore more vulnerable to detection. On account of this critical factor in the potential success or failure of a given mission, the British were understandably eager to incorporate as many home-grown Frenchmen into their Special Operations sector as possible.

Standing at attention in de Gaulle's office, nineteen year-old Robert De La Rochefoucauld waited breathlessly while his future hung in the balance.

General de Gaulle gazed at me for a moment; then, with the hauteur for which he was so widely renowned, he announced to me his momentous decision: "Even an alliance with the Devil himself would be acceptable if undertaken for the glory of France. I wish you the very best of luck!" Through the many decades that have passed since I experienced this defining moment in my life, the words of this long-awaited response have remained forever imprinted in the recesses of my conscious mind.[7]

It is not difficult to visualise the tall, lanky young Frenchman leaving the Carlton Gardens Headquarters in late 1942 with a distinct spring in his step as he manoeuvred his way through the war-ravaged streets of London. His first priority was to contact his original mentor, Eric Picquet-Wicks, and report that he had received the green light from General de Gaulle himself. A dream come true!

A few days after my visit to Carlton Gardens, Major Picquet-Wicks, highly pleased with the results of my successful interview, introduced me to the French officer in charge of a particular section of the British Special Operations. The decision was then made to send me off to the SOE training facility.[8]

Without pulling any punches, it was made clear to me that the objective of this training period was to assess my aptitude for military life and specifically my aptitude for the type of combat in which commandos were required to engage. Frank and to-the-point, the redoubtable Major Picquet-Wicks made no bones about the importance of these four or five months of training and impressed upon me the fact that it would be exceptionally demanding. Should I prove incapable of withstanding the rigors involved, I would be im-mediately dispatched for service in a regular army unit. Did I detect a hint of humour in his description of what fate held in store for me should I fail to measure up? In retrospect, I rather suspect this was the case.[9]

In the interval, the commando-to-be was given a few days' leave. The end of the month of December was fast approach-ing and it seemed only right to bring on a bit of good cheer and forget the blackout by gathering a few friends together to celebrate Christmas and New Year's. De La Rochefoucauld notes that the German Luftwaffe invited itself along as well, so his holiday was enjoyed despite the threat of enemy bombs descending from a great height.[10]

A widely circulated flyer aimed towards all French citizens following de Gaulle's call-to-arms on the BBC in July 1941.

INSIGNE par le-
quel se recon-
nurent les pre-
miers « Fran-
çais libres » de
Londres.

Insignia worn by the original Free French Forces
in London as a sign of recognition.
Photo: Musée Leclerc, Paris.

A member of the Free French militia
stands guard at the entrance to
General Charles de Gaulle's London
headquarters at 1 Carlton Gardens.
Photo: Musée Leclerc, Paris.

6

THE MANY FACETS
OF SUBTERFUGE

Like so many of the young men who had volunteered for active military service, Robert De La Rochefoucauld now found himself poised on the threshold of a period in his life that would indelibly mark his future. Whether or not Major Piquet-Wicks had been speaking in jest about what would befall anyone who did not pass muster during the rigorous training that lay in store for all those recruited for service in the Special Operations Executive was anyone's guess. What was sometimes referred to as 'the Finishing School 'was clearly going to involve the ultimate test of both mental and physical endurance. What lay ahead was certainly not for the weak-kneed or wobbly!

Still, the training period started off rather gently with a battery of written tests which evidently posed no great difficulty for De La Rochefoucauld. Hard on the heels of this relatively civilized induction, the real training then began in earnest.[1]

> We were up at 6 a.m. sharp and our first thrill of the day
> consisted of a hike. For the first few days, it was set at three

63

miles with each of us carrying a twenty-five pound pack on our backs. But that was just to ease us in. Relatively soon, we progressed to stretches of fifteen and even twenty-mile gruelling stints hefting fifty pound packs over some very difficult terrain.

Then it was time for our introduction to parachute jumping. To begin with, we were dropped onto a trampoline from a height of six feet and learned the technique of landing in a somersault roll. After this introductory phase, we moved on to the real thing. Accompanied by a trainer, we were each sent up one-by-one in a balloon till we reached an altitude of roughly 500 feet. And all this was to be accomplished without displaying even a hint of hesitation. To be truthful, even to this day I have retained horrific memories of those practise jumps. The balloon was anchored to the ground by a rope, and—for reasons that still remain a mystery to me—this rope reinforced the sensation of a void, causing my head to spin in the most alarming fashion. It was vertigo at its unforgettable worst![2]

Another essential aspect of our training included an intensive course in the rudiments of military assault tactics. Loaded down with weapons and equipment, we had to learn to crawl on our stomachs and scale walls without detection. After having thrown and secured a grappling hook to the top of a building, we were required to make several ascents and descents before moving on to the next phase in perfecting our techniques as covert warriors.[3]

To impart these operations with a genuinely true-to-life flavour and discourage anyone from lagging behind, shots were fired from real weapons to keep the trainees on the move. It is not difficult to imagine the haste and enthusiasm for evasion displayed by the potential targets with the prospect of a hail of bullets aimed at their backsides.

And when it came to the use of firearms, as a matter of course, there was also detailed instruction and practice in the use of a full range of weaponry including pistols, revolvers, rifles, sub-machine guns and Sten guns. But, of necessity, for the future infiltrators it was also essential to become familiar with the use of every type of weapon found in the enemy arsenal. Once he was back in France operating in the field, on more than one occasion this particular aspect of his training would later serve De La Rochefoucauld extremely well. Without it, his life-span might well have been substantially shortened.

Training in the use of explosives was also incorporated into the meticulously planned SOE agenda. As future saboteurs, De La Rochefoucauld and his fellow trainees became initiated into the delicate art of blowing up a bridge, railway tracks, electrical pylons, and—needless to say—they also learned how to avoid blowing themselves up in the process.

When it came to learning the tricks of the trade in hand-to-hand combat, we were introduced to every aspect of the martial arts, including not only judo and karate, but beyond this, to the exact method required to kill a man without using any weapon other than the flat of the hand. We had to learn, as well, how to achieve the same result with a knife.

Undoubtedly this would have involved the use of a standard Commando issue Fairbairn–Sykes stiletto or double-edged knife—an essential weapon for use in hand-to-hand combat.[4]

In a slightly less deadly vein came the teaching of the necessary skills for opening a locked door, window or even a safe. The British—ever mindful of employing the expertise of nothing but the best—had arranged for the release from prison of a select number of accomplished thieves who, as our instructors, then brought the benefit of their particular knowledge and experience to the uninitiated.

And just when we began to think we had been put through all our paces, the final stages of our training still held some surprises in store for us. Several times we were parachuted at daybreak into the middle of the countryside without any documents. The object of the exercise was to make it back to camp, eluding all the military police surveillance teams which had been charged with the task of intercepting us. It goes almost without saying that sooner or later quite a few of us were apprehended, but by no means everyone.[5]

On one occasion, De La Rochefoucauld and a few companions made it back into camp with bare torsos and clad only in sweaty undershorts after having traversed some twenty or thirty miles and making their own athletic fashion statement. Whenever anyone of the group spotted a suspicious figure or vehicle in the distance, this became the signal to begin flailing about making vigorous callisthenic-style movements accompanied by deep breathing exercises. To all intents and purposes these chaps appeared to be nothing more than a bunch of enthusiastic young athletes engaged in fitness training, which—as it happened—was not all that far from the truth. But in the process of executing their ingenious ruse, they had managed to evade detection, which was, after all, the object of the exercise.

Another adventure evokes an even pleasanter memory: I was dropped by parachute with a companion who had the misfortune of badly twisting his ankle on landing. Since he could not walk, it was our good fortune to discover an unattended

Military Police car in the vicinity and make off with it. To the utter astonishment of everyone in camp, we made our unexpected entrance, having covered a fair number of miles behind the wheel of this vehicle and arrived back scarcely four hours later. Unfortunately, there were no prizes awarded for speed and ingenuity, however those responsible for the exercise had to admit that the successful completion of our assignment had been a demonstration of quick-witted audacity as well as an obvious ability to take advantage of an unexpected situation.

Throughout these assorted adventures and misadventures, our training progressed. Subconsciously—in and of themselves—even our conversations within the group and with our instructors contributed to our psychological state of preparedness. One of the most vital elements of our final preparation for the realities of work in the field was the acquisition of the techniques we would require in the event of having to submit to an interrogation. In order to withstand the rigours of this dreaded eventuality, it was essential for each of us to be armed with the knowledge of what to expect. This particular aspect of our training was also something which later turned out to be especially useful to me on more than one occasion.

At the same time, the intensity of the rigorous training we underwent over a prolonged period guaranteed that we were in the best possible condition for what lay ahead. In hindsight, I think our experiences during these long and exacting months of preparation could be summed up by concluding that the main objective of our training had been to turn us into resourceful young replicas of the future Agent 007.[6]

While, at first glance, this comparison to the legendary figure of James Bond may appear somewhat tenuous, there are extenuating circumstances that could offer a plausible degree of substance to these remarks. The fact that 007's post-war creator, former Royal Navy Commander, Ian Fleming, spent the duration of the War Years embroiled in every imaginable aspect of covert intelligence activities may, in fact, lend a certain validity to De La Rochefoucauld's retrospective observation.[7]

In any event, what had begun five months earlier as a motley group of roughly thirty trainees had been pared down to a final seven or eight who were the successful candidates deemed suitably qualified for service in the "active" branch of the top-secret organization known as the Special Operations Executive (SOE). And among their number was Robert De La Rochefoucauld, the French recruit who had been put through his paces and proven he was made of "the right stuff". He notes that those who failed to make the grade were subsequently enlisted for service in the regular militia and there is a good chance that he was recalling the initial warning issued to him in jest by Major Eric Piquet-Wicks when he first set off into this unknown and secret world.

> By June 1943, those of us who had made it through the previous five months and come out the other side were champing at the bit to embark on our first mission. I was not far short of my twentieth birthday, and at that moment, I confess to feeling that these were truly the best days of my life. Had I not arrived safely in England after a roller-coaster series of events dictated by fate and circumstances? Was I not on the brink of realizing my most fervent patriotic dreams, buoyed by the knowledge that before long the particulars of my immediate future would become specific? The details of our first mission were finally taking shape almost exactly one year before D-Day.

On the night of our departure, we were given a bracing send-off by an SOE colonel whose parting words reminded us that we were not being sent on this assignment to lose our lives but to accomplish a specific and vitally important mission. He then finished off his heartening expression of encouragement by telling us he was counting on seeing us back in England in short order.[8]

False Identity papers used by SOE agent Robert De La Rochefoucauld in the name of Rene Lallier while operating in Occupied France. (recto) Courtesy the De La Rochefoucauld family archives.

False Identity papers used by SOE agent Robert De La
Rochefoucauld while operating in Occupied France. (verso)
Courtesy the De La Rochefoucauld family archives.

7

THE DROP ZONE

It goes almost without saying that the degree of organization and painstaking planning that preceded the successful infiltration of every agent assigned to covert operations in Nazi-occupied Europe was incredibly complex. When it came to total preparedness for a mission, absolutely nothing could be left to chance. The SOE section charged with providing the required support for its operatives developed its own extensive laundry list of essentials such as the provision of weapons and explosives, as well as the all-important radio transmitter that could be concealed in a suitcase. This same 'support' department was also responsible for forging all the necessary passes, identity cards and ration documents, and it even extended to the precise duplication of European-style watches, clothing and shoes complete with authentic labels. Each and every detail—no matter how small—could prove vital to an agent's survival.[1]

The Control Tower at top-secret Tempsford airfield in
Bedfordshire from which SOE agents were flown by
moonlight to and from designated landing sites in Occupied
Europe from 1941—1945. Photo credit: Peter Haining.

Essentially, however, there were limited options in terms of the
actual means of effecting safe and undetected infiltrations and ex-
tractions from a full range of hush-hush locations. And whether the
actual means of conveyance was by sea or by air, neither option was
without its own specific hazards at the appointed hour—not the least
of these being prevailing winds and weather, to say nothing of detection by the enemy or by the ever-present reality of betrayal.

In order to infiltrate its agents into Nazi-Occupied territory
by air, the vast majority of SOE missions to France utilized RAF
Tempsford—an ultra-secret airfield situated in the countryside not
far from Cambridge.[2]. Parachute drops would be scheduled for the
pre-dawn hours on a clear moonlit night in order to ensure opti-
mum conditions for the pilots to locate their target without difficulty.

Detection by an enemy fighter could never be ruled out, but for the most part, Lady Luck prevailed.[3]

I learned that I was to be dropped by parachute over the Morvan—a mountainous region located in central France—accompanied by two Englishmen, one of whom was the radio-operator who would be responsible for maintaining contact with our British controllers. Those in charge of planning for the operation had already arranged for the local cell or réseau of the French underground network to pick us up from a pre-arranged location after the drop. The main purpose of our mission was to provide on-the-spot training to members of these local Resistance groups in the use of explosives.

Our task was to teach them the essential techniques for creating effective acts of sabotage, whether the target was a power plant, railway tracks or lines of communication. In essence, it was up to us to instigate and assist in any possible activity that could be aimed at foiling or slowing down the efficiency and smoothness of German operations on French soil. In essence, our mission was to confound the enemy at every turn. And so it came to pass that within a few short hours, my status was transformed from pupil to the role of instructor armed with all the tools of the trade.[4]

Following a two a.m. take-off, once the aircraft had made its way safely across the Channel, it suddenly became the target of a sudden 'flack' fusillade let loose by German artillery batteries defending the French coast. For De La Rochefoucauld—and possibly also for his two companions on the mission—this enemy action was his baptism by fire. Fortunately, it turned out to be a relatively short-lived period of heart-pounding fear that left only a few souvenir dents on the plane's exterior and a handful of slightly shaken but unbruised passengers in its wake. Once over this initial salvo, the flight proceeded without incident and the mission's radio-operator established contact with the local *maquis* who were responsible for organizing the 'reception committee' at the drop zone.[5]

They, of course, had been put on alert to be in readiness for the new arrivals and were no doubt already in position, listening for the distant drone of a low-flying aircraft.

After our plane had made two passes over the pre-arranged drop zone, we were able to pick out a triangle of lights flashing below. This was the customary signal to indicate that everything was in readiness for our arrival. As we sat waiting for the signal to prepare to jump, the door at the side of the aircraft was pulled opened, and for a few tense moments our feet were left dangling in empty space. Each of us had been assigned the precise order in which we would jump and I found myself at the head of the line. Already the 'dispatcher'—the crew member responsible for supervising the jump—had placed himself behind me. Above us, there was a light on which our eyes remained fixed: red, no one was to move; green, the designated jumper was to hurtle off into the unknown. The flashing red light—according to our instructions—signalled that my equipment bag was to be pitched out. This contained my weapons and other gear, and was attached to my belt by a strap about thirty feet long. I was to jump immediately afterwards, assisted by the 'jump master' who was also responsible for seeing that the parachutes did not get snagged onto part of the aircraft.

Fortunately, I landed without any problems, as did both my two companions. After folding up our parachutes and recovering our equipment, we were welcomed by a group of about ten men—all of whom belonged to the local maquis réseau. Within minutes, they had loaded us and our equipment into a light truck, and we sped away from the drop zone to avoid the possibility that the Germans had spotted the plane's passage and were already attempting to hunt us down. After an hour on the road, we reached a wooded area, south of Avallon, near the village of Quarré-les-Tombes, named after the historic Gallo-Roman tombstones grouped around its church.[6]

About twenty men were gathered at Quarré-les-Tombes awaiting our arrival and introductions were made all around. Convinced of the goodwill engendered by bearing small gifts for such occasions, we generously distributed the cigarettes and chocolate we had brought with us for this express purpose. The leader of this particular réseaux was a man of forty or so, known as 'The Pope' and he gave a us a very cordial welcome. For one reason or another, he had evidently chosen to use the name Pious VII as his nom de guerre.

During the course of our ensuing conversation, he did not fail to emphasize his determination to strike a blow against the Germans at the earliest opportunity, however he was quick to point out his concerns about the serious lack of resources they were facing. In response, I was pleased to be able to outline to him the nature of our mission, which was to offer him every possible assistance, to train his men in the use of explosives and, if need be, to obtain additional resources for him.

Our first priority was to take a quick inventory of all the arms and munitions currently in their possession. That was completed in short order and it was plain to see that his concerns were well founded. Their supply of arms and ammunition was pathetically inadequate. It seemed to us that the best course of action would be to ask those in charge of our mission to obtain a parachute drop of additional supplies from a reliable source. Our radio-operator then made contact with London and was told that the answer to our request would be radioed back two days later at precisely the same time.

By dint of good fortune, within two days the reply came back punctually at the agreed time: Yes, we should expect a supplementary parachute drop at the same location where we had originally landed. Six containers of explosives and individual weapons would be included. But, to our great frustration, the date and time of this operation was not specified. We were then instructed to make radio contact daily at the same time in order that these vital details could be communicated to us.[7]

Two long and tedious weeks of endless waiting by the wireless went by before the radio message of confirmation from London finally came through. The drop was scheduled to take place the following day at 4 a.m. With one of the maquisards at the wheel of the truck, the group left their hiding place under cover of darkness and arrived undetected at the drop zone. The lights were set up and the radio-operator waited in readiness to establish contact with the aircraft as soon as it appeared. As luck would have it, the plane's arrival was well- timed. While they were in the process of setting up the lights, it made its first pass overhead. Then, at an altitude of about 500 feet, it completed its second fly-over and dropped the precious containers directly on target. The containers were trundled off on the double and the parachutes folded in all possible haste. It was never a good idea to linger unnecessarily at the scene of a parachute drop.

Once they had arrived at a more secure place in a wooded area, they took a rapid inventory of what had been dropped from the heavens. And what a fine surprise awaited them as they hastily unpacked the contents of the bonanza; a good supply of weapons including a number of submachine-guns, a sufficient quantity of plastique explosive, chocolate and cigarettes. In short, all that was required to prepare for action!

Now that the group had been suitably equipped, there was no time to lose. The training of the band of maquisards in the intricacies of clandestine warfare could begin immediately—if not sooner. Within the next few weeks, the novice trainees became increasingly proficient with each passing day and by the end of August, dealing with explosives no longer held any secrets for them. They were now ready to undertake a mission of utmost importance. The destruction of a specific target that would seriously hamper German military activity for some time to come.

At the beginning of September, we were busy formulating our plan to blow up the power plant that provided electricity not only to the city of Avallon but also to a large factory designated for repairs to German equipment. After many reconnaissance missions and a thorough scouting of the site, we proceeded to successfully set the wheels of sabotage in motion.

To our considerable satisfaction, everything came off according to plan. The Avallon power plant was completely destroyed, the pylons flattened, and the factory assigned for repairs to German military equipment rendered inoperable. Small wonder that we finished this operation with a sense of a pride in a job well done!

While waiting for the rapidly approaching moment when my two British companions and myself were due to be picked up by plane and flown back to England, we even managed to work in a few more small-scale operations by blowing up a few railway tracks in the vicinity.[8]

But occasionally things do not turn out quite as expected. Less than two months later, at the beginning of November 1943, De La Rochefoucauld was denounced by an unidentified traitor and taken prisoner by the Germans with the assistance of the local Milice.[9] Someone, for reasons that will remain forever unknown, had tipped off the authorities leaving Robert De La Rochefoucauld to their not-so-tender mercies.

Young Maquisards in France receive training in the use of weapons dropped in to Occupied France by the SOE.
Photo credit: Collection of Les Jeunes Maquisards.

8

BETRAYAL, TORTURE
AND ESCAPE

Betrayal again! And for the second time. The first potential arrest had only been averted through the good offices of the patriotic postal employee in Villeneuve two years earlier—the man who had alerted the De La Rochefoucauld family to the fact that Robert had been denounced to the Gestapo by someone in the vicinity. It was, in fact, this very warning that had precipitated his initial contact with the Resistance in Paris and his eventual passage through the Underground network and into Spain.

This time, having been apprehended without warning and kept under lock and key at the local Gestapo Headquarters, the possibility of escape would pose an entirely different combination of fortitude and ingenuity—accompanied by the unforeseen hand of Fate.

Legendary hero of the French
Resistance, Jean Moulin, (Max) who
died courageously in July 1943 after
being betrayed to the Gestapo in
Lyon. Photo courtesy of Musée Jean
Moulin, Paris.

Just six months prior to this reprehensible betrayal, at about the
same time as De La Rochefoucauld was about to set off from England
on his first SOE mission in June 1943, another French patriot had
suffered the same fate and paid for it with his life. Jean Moulin, the
great hero of the French Resistance, the man personally delegated
by de Gaulle to organize and co-ordinate the work of the 'Army of
the Shadows', had been denounced and fallen into the clutches of
the Gestapo's notorious Klaus Barbie in Lyon. Although tortured un-
mercifully at the hands of his captors, "Max" is said to have given
nothing and no one away.

When handed a piece of paper to reveal the names of associates,
he responded by substituting one of his signature cartoons depicting
an image of his sadistic tormentor. This, of course, resulted in further brutality to the point where Barbie's superiors ordered that Jean

Moulin be hospitalized in Germany. At the time of his death—the direct result of the injuries he sustained while in Barbie's custody—he was being transported by train to an unknown destination near Frankfurt. Jean Moulin, too, had been the victim of a treacherous betrayal, but he had left his countrymen with a legacy of honour that lives on to this day.[1]

The denunciation of Robert De La Rochefoucauld came six months later just as he was awaiting details of his extraction back to England with the other two British operatives.

One night, in a barn near Quarré-les-Tombes, I was in a deep sleep on a pile of hay. Without warning, I found myself being rudely awakened by at least ten men representing the Gestapo and the Milice. By way of a greeting, they started off with some well-aimed kicks, jabs and punches before binding me up like a sausage. They then began a thorough search of the barn, and went to untold lengths before finally locating one small cache of weapons. Not unexpectedly, I protested that I had no knowledge whatsoever of these weapons. I was playing the role of the ignorant country bumpkin to the hilt, however not quite well enough to convince them to believe me.

Dawn had barely broken when we rolled up in front of the Auxerre prison, a medieval-style little fort situated on the way out of town.[2] During the following days of incarceration, I underwent a series of increasingly intensive interrogations. It was exactly the sort of unpleasant experience that had been so fortuitously foreseen during the course of our preparatory psychological training as future British agents operating in Nazi-occupied Europe.

Among the tactics for withstanding interrogation that we had learned—even in the event of torture—was that the best defence was to react with a violent display of anger towards the interrogators... to face them down with a totally unexpected offensive. With the resulting adrenaline rush which increases in intensity by feeding on itself, one no longer feels the pain of the blows being inflicted quite as intensely, and the temptation to divulge information tends to diminish or even disappear.

In this particular case, my captors incessantly hurled accusations at me insisting that I was both a Communist and an agitator. Responding in tones that equalled theirs in volume, I replied that "not all Communists were agitators, but that all agitators were Communists" and that I was neither one nor the other! I must admit that sometime after the war, when I had long since forgotten having made this particular allegation about Communists, a former French prison guard with a long memory reminded me of it.

In addition, my interrogators were also insistent on repeatedly demanding that I reveal the identity of Pious VII. (This was the nom de guerre of the head of the Maquis réseau which had welcomed me on my arrival in France that summer.) Without hesitation, I repeatedly responded by telling them that this was the name of a Pope during the reign of Napoleon. Not surprisingly, they were disinclined to believe my explanation, and were, in fact, convinced that I was attempting to make fun of them—a conclusion which, admittedly, was not entirely off the mark!

Eventually, after four months, they despaired of getting any useful information out of me, and—like so many before me—I was summarily brought before a German military tribunal. Without any legal representation, the verdict was forthcoming within minutes. I had been condemned to death in the same manner as any other French Resistance fighter would be. I was to be taken before a firing squad and shot.[3]

Clearly, events were taking on a decidedly serious turn. Early one morning, not long after his excuse for a trial, De La Rochefoucauld was visited by a German priest, and although the man spoke not a word of French, it was far from difficult to interpret the significance of his presence in the prisoner's cell.

Not long after receiving the priest's blessing, the man known as René Lallier, accompanied by another unfortunate Resistance captive who had been relegated to the same fate, was shoved into the back of a truck, in which two coffins had already been placed in readiness for use within the hour. For some inexplicable reason, neither of the prisoners had been handcuffed. Perhaps the ominous presence of the coffins plus that of two armed guards was considered a sufficiently adequate deterrent to any possible thoughts of escape.

Once inside the truck, the guards indicated that the prisoners should each make themselves at home on one or other of the two coffins; but, for some reason, instead of heading out into the countryside, the truck was driven into the centre of the town of Auxerre. At this point it was about 8 o'clock and the traffic in town almost non-existent. De La Rochefoucauld retains a vivid memory of the Charlie-Chaplinesque events that followed as they rattled through town towards their final destination.

Sitting there perched on my own coffin, I don't believe I was thinking of anything in particular, when suddenly I was seized by the realization that the moment of truth was upon me: I had to escape: Escape at all costs! In my present situation, there was no risk greater to avoid than the one that awaited me within the hour. All of this came to me in a blinding flash and without a moment's hesitation I said to my companion in misfortune: "Well, if I'm going to be shot, I prefer to be shot while attempting to escape. I'm going to make a run for it!"

"Are you out of your mind? "came his reply. "You'll never make it!!"

But I barely heard him. Operating entirely on instinct, I lunged towards the back of the truck and shoved the guards aside, before taking a giant leap towards freedom. By dint of great good fortune, I landed on my feet after performing a perfect somersault roll. The agility acquired thanks to the relentless parachute training at Ringway Camp had been successfully put to the ultimate test.

At the same time, the two guards in the truck had reacted quickly, shouldering their rifles and firing desperately in my direction, but on hearing the shots, the driver had immediately reacted by jamming on the brakes and this had sent the guards reeling.

Having escaped miraculously unscathed, I began zigzagging at top speed, taking the first street to my right, then the first to my left, in the desperate hope of throwing off pursuit. To make matters worse, the town was totally unfamiliar to me, so it was hopeless for me to try to locate a possible refuge at l'hôtel de La Fontaine. The owner—a Resistance member— had earlier brought me some food packages to the prison, alleging that I was a member of his family. But how was I to find his hotel and avoid my pursuers at the same time? Better just to continue trying to elude them and hope for the best.[4]

As the now desperate fugitive rounded a corner, he found himself in front of a large villa—festooned with Swastikas which identified it as the local Gestapo Headquarters. Badly winded after his escape on the run and loathe to draw further attention to himself, he made a valiant attempt to slow to a casual walk while passing the villa. Near the entrance, De La Rochefoucauld noticed a sleek black Citroën bearing the red and black pennant signifying that this vehicle had been assigned to an officer of the Reich. He also caught sight of the driver pacing up and down puffing on a cigarette to kill time while waiting for his high-ranking passenger to emerge.

Continuing past the vehicle, De La Rochefoucauld cast a cautious sideways glance into the courtyard and observed that the key was still in the Citroën's ignition. At the same time, he could hear frantic shouting in the distance and was left in little doubt that his pursuers were hot on his heels. The window of opportunity was closing fast. Given the distance from the chauffeur at that moment, there was at least a slim chance that he could make it to the car door and then pray that it had been left unlocked. Sure enough, when he yanked the handle towards him, the door swung open and within seconds he had slipped into the driver's seat.

The key offered no resistance and the engine started after a quarter-turn, however the ensuing roar of the engine instantly captured the attention of the chauffeur, who immediately took in the situation and fired off a badly-aimed shot. Almost certainly this gross negligence of duty would soon be rewarded by a hasty transfer to a hardship posting. This eventuality, however, was the last thing on the mind of the lucky man at the wheel of that German staff car.

I crisscrossed through the city at top speed, having no idea where to go and how to get out of town. Finally I spotted a sign indicating the route to Paris and veered off in that directions. Irony of ironies, the route took me right back past the prison I had left only an hour earlier—little imagining at the time that I would ever lay eyes on it again. In a few minutes I was driving at a good clip along a main highway astonishingly alive and well to say nothing of overjoyed at this glorious taste of freedom.

With my hands planted firmly on the wheel, I was struck by the recurring thought that a car is definitely more comfortable than a coffin. As I rolled merrily on down the highway, the world was indeed my private oyster! The Citroen had a full tank of petrol and, looking out at the officer's pennant with its Swastika, I was thoroughly enjoying the humour of the situation. It looked as I could be almost certain of arriving in Paris without difficulty.

Sadly, this turned out to be a snare and a delusion. From Auxerre, all the telephone lines were in perfect working order and the alarm had been sounded for the entire surrounding area. After about a dozen or so miles of carefree travel, just ahead I spotted a roadblock, two well-armed soldiers, and across the road, a wooden barrier on two trestles.

I slowed down, shifted into second gear, and then floored the accelerator. The wooden barrier flew into the air, along with one of the Germans. The second fellow immediately started firing and the bullets made a few holes in the car, but nothing major. As soon I could, I took the first dirt road on my left. By now, as a result of the impact, the engine was smoking.

The radiator had been damaged. Bouncing over washboard ruts, I finally arrived at a spot near a quarry where I decided it would definitely be in my best interests to abandon the vehicle. Just at the edge of the quarry, I got out, gave my failing transportation a good push and watched it crash dramatically to the bottom. One less vehicle for the Reich![5]

Disappearing into the first wooded area he came to, De La Rochefoucauld had no choice but to cool his heels while waiting impatiently for nightfall. Once again, with no idea where he was or where he should go, he found himself at a total loss. After dark he began walking aimlessly for an hour or two, possibly more, until he realized he was approaching a large town. Before long, a sign on the road revealed the name. Auxerre! Irony of ironies, he had come full circle.

It was then that I decided to make use of the one resource I had not been able to call on that morning when I was on the run through the streets of Auxerre. One of the two good local hotels, l'Hôtel de la Fontaine was situated in the centre of town, close to the post office building. In those days, its owner was a member of the Resistance and during my imprisonment, it was he who had kindly arranged for deliveries of food for me.

I decided that I should try to contact him by telephone, but first I had to locate a kiosk. Not something to be found on every street corner. Taking a thousand and one precautions to try to make myself invisible, I slipped into town at nightfall. The darkness brought reassurance and silence to the city. But still there was no kiosk to be found!

Fortunately, I spied a general store that had not yet locked up for the night. I entered and asked for permission to use the telephone. After looking up the number in the telephone book, very conscious of the fact that I was playing one of my last cards, I placed the call. Foiled again! I was informed that the hotel owner had already left for the night. And in this situation, leaving any kind of message was completely out of the question. What to do?

Once again it was time for me to gamble on taking an enormous risk. I seized the poor grocer by the shoulders and naturally, his reaction was one of utter dismay. Perhaps he had a lunatic on his hands? But before he had the chance to call out to anyone, I asked him one crucial and defining question:

"Are you good Frenchman?

"But, of course, I am a good Frenchman!"

That was all I needed to hear. After this, there was no longer any need to hesitate.

"I have just escaped," I told him, "And I am being pursued by the Germans"

"Well, that explains a lot," came his reply. "So it's because of you that there has been such an uproar in town since this morning? But you are in luck, my friend: I will take you in!"[6]

The patriotic grocer's name was M. Séguinot and he immediately introduced their visitor to his wife. Madame at once embraced him warmly and then proceeded to busy herself in the kitchen. Before

BETRAYAL, TORTURE AND ESCAPE

long, she had served up a delicious and bountiful meal—all the while explaining to him how—in case of danger or a house-search by the Germans or the Milice—he could make a quick and hopefully undetected get-away out the back door.[7]

This kind and hospitable soul then escorted their unexpected overnight guest into bed with her father, a paralytic old man, who could neither speak a word nor move a muscle. Settled in beside such a peaceful companion, the exhausted runaway immediately fell into a deep and dreamless sleep. And small wonder, after a day that had begun at the crack of dawn with a prisoner's last visit from a German priest to be followed in quick succession by an unimaginable series of heart-stopping adventures that even James Bond would be hard-pressed to survive!

The following day, he asked his gracious host, M. Séguinot, if he would go to the Hôtel de La Fontaine, and—with all possible discretion—ask to see the owner in person, to explain what fate had left on his doorstep. That same evening, the hotel owner appeared at the grocery store. The two men fell into each other's arms and the hotelier announced that he had brought clothes and, better still, that he had devised a plan of escape.

He explained that the walls of Auxerre were already plastered with posters bearing the photograph of the wanted fugitive, Rene Lallier, and that it was imperative that De La Rochefoucauld should leave town as soon as the coast was clear. It seemed the better part of caution, however, to wait two or three days for the hue and cry to die down before putting his plan into action.

In the meantime, he could also arrange to provide a new identity card. What's more, as the proprietor of a hotel, he was allowed to keep his vehicle equipped with a gas generator, as well as carry a permit to operate it. His plan was to take the escapee in the truck and let him out near a small town where he would board a train bound for Paris.

Two days later, according to plan, the vehicle drew to a halt in front of the grocery store and the passenger climbed into the back, where he promptly hid himself behind sacks and bales of hay destined for the hotel-keeper's herd of sheep.

Just outside town, we were stopped by a barrier, manned by soldiers with whom the customary dialogue ensued:

"Papers!"

"Here is my pass.

"Where are you going?

"To feed my sheep for my hotel. I am the owner of l'Hôtel de La Fontaine in Auxerre.

"Hôtel de La Fontaine, Très bon", ventured the soldier, although in all likelihood he had never darkened the hotel's door. He then proceeded to saunter around to the back of the truck, poked his bayonet into a bale or two of hay and gave us the OK sign. We could be on our way. A stroke of luck in our hour of need!

In due course, we finally arrived at the little station and the end of my ride with just five minutes to spare before the departure of the train for Paris. The timing could not have been better. My chauffeur left the truck and hurried to the wicket to buy me a ticket in third class. Our plan was already in place. When the train came chugging into the station, I would emerge from the truck, and he would hand me the ticket.

Clutching the ticket, I ran to join the line-up of other travellers; a railway employee punched my ticket and I climbed aboard. The compartment I chose was crammed to the hilt—to the point that the wooden slats with which third class carriages were equipped at that time, were not even visible. That, however, was the least of my worries, I was desperate for the departure of the train. When it finally started to move forward, I assumed I was finally out of danger—but, alas, nothing is ever that simple.[8]

The next stop was a small station at Laroche-Migennes. Looking out the window, De La Rochefoucauld could see that the platform was overflowing with policemen and German soldiers. The same was true of the other platform for trains headed in the opposite direction. Turning to his neighbour, a travelling salesman, he inquired whether the fellow knew why there were so many police and military about. His reply was that he had absolutely no idea, but that the situation had been the same for the past three days.

That piece of information was more than enough for De La Rochefoucauld to understand perfectly what this was all about. When he went out into the corridor, he could see that at either end of the carriage there was a soldier methodically checking the passengers' papers. Clearly, he would have to come up with a plan to avoid this at all costs as he was not entirely confident about the false identity card which had been given to him by his Resistance friend. Would the document stand up to close scrutiny? When it came to checking identity papers, the German were meticulous to a fault. For an agent having credible papers in one's possession was the key to self-preservation and he suspected it would only be asking for trouble to present the forged card for inspection. His only recourse would be to hide... and in all possible haste.

By dint of good fortune, the old pre-war railway cars had toilets situated in the centre of each carriage. Taking advantage of the moment when the German closest to him had gone into a compartment, he managed to slip into the WC. Once inside, he folded himself accordion-like into a ball and squeezed under the washbasin behind the door he had purposely left unlocked. And just as he had hoped: when the door swung open, he was successfully hidden from view. The soldier completed his cursory check and moved on.

> Ten minutes later, assuming that the coast was clear, I stood up to get out of my cramped hiding place. I had been well and truly petrified—to the point where I was covered in perspiration. After washing my face, I returned to my seat feeling more than a little shaken by the events of the day.

> At last, without any further unnerving incidents, the train arrived three hours later at the Gare de Lyon—the northern terminus of the Paris–Marseille railway. Hiding under the basin had been the final test for my almost shattered nerves. As I felt the station platform beneath my feet, I was suddenly overcome by a glorious sensation of euphoria. I had actually made good my escape and was breathing in the scents and smells of freedom! Then came an involuntary burst of maniacal laughter—to the point where people turned to look at me with pity in their eyes. Poor fellow! Another of the world's growing multitude of madmen on the loose...[9]

Recently brought to light, this photograph taken by an unidentified
German soldier secretly captured the executions of French
Resistance captives at Mont-Valerien on 21 February 1941.
Photo credit: *The Daily Mail.*

9

INTERLUDE IN PARIS

All too quickly, the brief period of elation over the hapless fugitive's safe arrival at the Gare de Lyon began to look and feel somewhat less than joyful. Night was falling and it was miserably cold. To compound the situation, although he had papers which he could only hope were more or less in order, when it came to the matter of money, his pockets were completely empty.

Yet another dilemma to contend with and he had barely set foot outside the station! Where could he be certain that he would be in good hands and warm at the same time? The answer surfaced almost at once. He would make his way on foot to the other end of Paris, to the home of his 'Uncle Gotz', who was married to his mother's cousin. Over the years, whenever he had visited Paris, their house on Rue Paul-Baudry had become like a second home to him. For their part, the childless couple had long since adopted young Robert as the son they never had. De La Rochefoucauld remembered:

I rang the doorbell and Geoffroy Gotz himself opened the door. Despite my strained and emaciated appearance, aided and abetted by the unfamiliar eye-glasses I was wearing as an attempt at disguise, he recognized me at once and I was ushered in with a welcoming embrace.He was totally taken aback, of course. What on earth was I doing in Paris? Had I not been arrested and detained somewhere by the Germans?

He propelled me towards the living room where my aunt, seated in an armchair, was working on some embroidery. I was immediately struck by the timeless peace and serenity of the scene before me. She raised her eyes in amazement, then rose to greet me with open arms. For me, this was a long-treasured moment. The rush of relief and absolute joy at finding myself here—alive and embraced in this warm and loving home—was almost indescribable. It was only later that thoughts of the possible danger I might be exposing them to for providing shelter to a fugitive from the firing squad entered my head.

During the course of the next hour or so, I retraced the kaleidoscopic events that had completely changed my life, beginning in 1942 with my departure for Spain, my first imprisonment in Miranda, the flight from Madrid to England with Ambassador Hoare and my two RAF friends. Then came the tale of my parachute drop into the Morvan, my betrayal and subsequent capture by the Germans, a second imprisonment—infinitely worse than the Spanish experience—then the death sentence, and finally my escape. Hanging on my every word, my dear friends sat spellbound and speechless. At last my uncle broke the silence with the understatement of the evening: "Well then! We are indeed lucky to have you with us, are we not ?" How could I fail to agree?

In spite of rationing restrictions, when the time came, the dinner I was served seemed incredibly lavish and our conversation continued in a highly animated fashion. Later, when overcome by fatigue, I found it close to impossible to imagine the sense of nostalgia I felt—finding myself back in the bedroom where I had spent so many nights as an adolescent. So very few years had passed since then, yet for me, it was now another age, another time, another life. I lay there on the edge of sleep marvelling at my incredible luck.[1]

The next day, late in the morning, De La Rochefoucauld awoke to the sight of an enormous and decidedly welcome breakfast. Uncle Geoffroy had left the house earlier to put in a telephone call to Robert's parents at Villeneuve. For security reasons he had taken the wise precaution of placing the call from a post office. Given the temper of the times, it was always best to err on the side of caution. On his return, he announced that he had been able to reach them and pass on the good news.

They were, of course, overjoyed and promised to be in Paris the next day. Then—much after the fact—Robert would finally learn more about his father's release from Stalag XVIIIA which had occurred sometime after his own enforced odyssey from Villeneuve early in 1942.

Feeling refreshed and exhilarated after a long and dreamless sleep, that afternoon he telephoned a friend who immediately invited him for a drink at her home on Constantine Street, near Les Invalides. The whole family was there to extend an exuberant welcome and ply him with excellent food and other delicacies. Their generosity also extended to the provision of ration tickets followed by invitations for meals in their home to help lighten the drain on the food resources of his aunt and uncle. As De La Rochefoucauld would later write in his memoir, "Only people who lived through these dark days could begin to imagine the stringencies of food rationing at that time and appreciate the true value of such largesse."

The following day heralded the arrival of his parents in Paris. To be so unexpectedly reunited at long last with his beloved mother and father made for a highly emotional reunion. However, once the initial excitement had subsided, Robert realized that, in all fairness, he really must raise the difficult subject of his plans for the future. As delicately as possible, he explained that he felt duty bound to leave for England as soon as he had regained his strength and rid himself of the nasty case of scabies he had brought with him as a less-than-welcome souvenir of those two months spent in the Auxerres prison.

My mother, who never lost her sense of the practical, had already planned a complete program of recuperation for me. She suggested that we get in touch with a dear cousin, Gabriel de Mortemart, who lived in a charming village outside Paris. When contacted, M. de Mortemart instantly agreed to take me in, despite the risks my presence could entail, And so it was settled that I should go to Saint-Vrain at the beginning of the following week.

In the days preceding my departure, my every wish was fully indulged. In fact, this brief period of my life is especially imprinted in my memory since it fell so unexpectedly between two series of events that were far removed from the loving care lavished upon me by my parents, relatives and friends.

Thanks to the medical intervention of a friend of the Gotz cousins, I managed to be rid of the last of my 'jailbird' scabies and spent much of my time devouring the sort of food I had lost the habit of enjoying. Dining alternately with the Murats, then with the Gotz', then with my parents, who were staying with my grandmother on La Motte-Piquet Avenue, I soon put on some of the weight I had lost while languishing in prison.

Mingling once again like this in Paris society, I could not fail to notice certain changes. Subtle changes, but ones that suggested a renewed sense of hope. Snatches of overheard conversation, unexpected silences, and people's facial expressions all gave me the distinct impression that belief in the possibility of an Allied victory was growing stronger by the day. Moreover, the requirements of the STO (Service du Travail Obligatoire) or Enforced Labour Service[2] imposed by the Nazi Occupation in 1942 and administered by the Vichy government was devastating many families.

A good number of these young fellows had preferred to go underground and join the Resistance rather than work in a German factory to further the enemy's war effort. In fact, it was the implementation of this ruling that helped to turn many young Frenchmen and their families into staunch supporters of the Free French and General de Gaulle.[3]

For some, outsmarting their oppressors became an almost irresistible challenge. In former SOE operative Philippe de Vomécourt's *France in Arms 1940-1945*, he writes of a beekeeper who happened to live just south of the original demarcation line, although his clover fields lay to the north of it, which necessitated his obtaining a permit to travel back and forth on a regular basis. The Germans also granted him authorization to take one workman along with him to assist in transporting the hives. When it came to the necessity of transporting downed British airmen who had been waiting in a 'safe house' until arrangements could be made to get them across the line into Vichy France and passed along the Resistance escape route, the permit proved more than useful , to say nothing of the bees.

Putting the hapless fliers into the back of his truck along with a load of beehives, the beekeeper drove southward until he was stopped at the line by a German soldier who carefully scrutinized his permit. At the sight of not one but four workmen in the truck, the German became agitated, which prompted M. Beekeeper to pull on a string just behind him that was attached to the lid of a hive.

As if on cue, out swarmed the bees, whereupon the guard flapped his arms frantically and waved them on shouting "Go! Go ! Go! Get out of here!" while making off to safety in the opposite direction. Once across the line, the beekeeper and his passengers were able to stop at the edge of a small wood where the airmen could hide, while the bees were once again restored to the hive. And, with any luck, the four 'workers' would soon be well on their way to freedom.

And as for the young fugitive regaiming his strength outside Paris…

The days I spent at Saint-Vrain were delightful. Gabriel de Mortemart welcomed me as a son, but as a precaution, had informed everyone else that he was taking in a trainee to do landscaping. He even insisted that his children call me "Monsieur." My major occupation, aside from trimming the hedges, was rambling about the countryside, eating well, and sleeping even better, but in spite of my restful surroundings, I had lost none of my determination to return to active service and the sooner, the better.

In Paris I had already made my presence known to a member of the Resistance who contacted London himself in order to facilitate my return. A meeting was arranged for the beginning of February and right on cue, a message came to Saint-Vrain that I was to return to Paris. On arrival, I made contact once again with the same person I had met with earlier and learned that I was to be smuggled out to England by submarine.

My instructions were that I should be in the vicinity of Calais on 25 February. The difficulty lay in the fact that access to the coast at that point was strictly forbidden and inside the 'Forbidden Access Zone', the Germans were exercising the strictest surveillance. Already rumour had it that this part of the coast had been designated for the landing of Allied troops. Clearly the area could only be penetrated in secret and with a well-laid plan in place.

The procedural instructions I was given resembled those I had followed for my crossing into Spain. The first step would involve contacting a member of the local Resistance group, whom I was to meet near the edge of a little village on the outskirts of Amiens. Minus a weapon and equipped only with a bicycle and a small amount of luggage, I boarded a train for Amiens. It was a local train, stopping in almost every little hamlet along the route, so I could get off at a small station located just short of Amiens, where—I reasoned—I was less likely to encounter the usual rigorous security checks. Something I wished to avoid at all costs!

It would also be safer to cycle on the less travelled country roads and avoid the main routes leading into Amiens. Having exited the train without any problems, I straddled my bike and set off to cover the ten miles which separated me from the designated village where I was to meet someone who answered to the name of Jean-Jacques and was a member of the local réseau whose code-name was Zéphir.[4]

Jean-Jacques assured De La Rochefoucauld that news of his Resistance activities and daring escape had preceded his arrival, and informed him that he, Jean-Jacques, along with members of his group, had received instructions that they were to assist him in getting aboard the submarine. He also explained that it would not be possible for this urgent exfiltration to take place anywhere near Calais, since the Germans had set up maximum surveillance along the entire coast in that region. The Germans were apprehensive that the anticipated Allied invasion force would land somewhere in the vicinity of Calais and had placed all troops on high alert. The rendez-vous with the submarine would therefore take place well south of Calais near the town of Berck-sur-mer[5] where German surveillance was relatively lighter.

Making frequent stops at pre-arranged locations known to Jean-Jacques, they met with various members of the Zéphir group and vital information was passed on concerning current German positions and troop movements, as well as the activities of enemy patrols. Once in possession of this intelligence, they could be assured of the best route to follow in order to arrive undetected at their ultimate destination.

Thanks to Zéphir, we arrived outside Berck without much difficulty on 27 February and made our way to a particular hiding place where five or six men had already gathered. Among them was an Englishman and also a Frenchman, who were waiting to hitch a ride on the same submarine that would hopefully transport all three of us back to England. Our hiding place was set up in a little copse a short distance inland from the coast along with a rubber dinghy of the type later known as a Zodiac which would convey the three of us out to the British submarine when the timing was right.

The pre-arranged course of action was that each night around one or two o'clock in the morning, a member of the Zéphir group would station himself on the shoreline with an electric flashlight and send a signal out to sea. Without a confirming response, no boarding attempt would take place, and the same procedure would have to be repeated the following night. If, however, the submarine responded with a signal back to us, we were make a mad dash for the shore, launch our dinghy, and paddle out in the dark to clamber aboard our safe passage to England. Little did I suspect what lay in store...[6]

10

SUBMARINE NIGHTMARE

For the SOE, the complexities of moving operatives in and out of France—or any other country in Occupied Europe, for that matter—were among its greatest challenges. When it came to planning and organizing the extraction of an agent, whether by aircraft or by vessel, the original coded message transmitted from France had to be received, decoded and passed on to the appropriate sector for approval before the wheels could even begin to be set in motion. Then, too, there was always the possibility that—despite every precaution—things could go awry.

By early 1944, the Germans had ruthlessly stepped up their already concerted efforts to locate and eradicate Resistance networks at every turn. Thanks to ever-expanding technology, the speed with which their mobile units could pick up a radio signal was nothing short of alarming. In addition, there were the never-diminishing difficulties brought on by traitorous betrayals, double-agents, nameless informers, and captives unable to withstand the brutal and relentless methods of extracting information to which they had routinely been subjected.

It was not without good cause, therefore, that operations such as the one in place for the extraction of De La Rochefoucauld from the appointed location near Berck were meticulously planned with painstaking attention to detail every step of the way.[1] And even then, unforeseen occurrences could always enter into the mix and create havoc.

The first attempt to rendez-vous with the promised submarine on 27 February—a moonless night—ended in disappointment. There was no response to our signal. We resigned ourselves to spending the following day waiting it in a wooded area while desperately attempting to bear the bitter cold that accompanied this particularly harsh winter. Keeping warm was a full-time occupation in itself.

The following night, 28 February relief, this time a return signal flashed back to us from offshore. It was action stations! Right on cue, we scrambled into our inflatable dinghy and paddled furiously out to sea. Luckily the sea was calm and within a quarter of an hour, just as we were beginning to grow apprehensive about our chances of locating the submarine, another signal made it possible for us to pinpoint its position.

Paddling towards it in the pitch dark, the submarine was almost invisible except for the vague outline of its conning tower. We had barely come in contact with its hull before the boarding drill was executed with lightning precision. And almost before we knew it, the sub began its silent descent beneath the surface.

What a strange sensation to suddenly find oneself ensconced in such totally unfamiliar surroundings! The commander welcomed us cordially; we were applauded by the crew and everyone exchanged congratulations and—on the part of my companions and myself—grateful thanks. We had barely arrived in the wardroom, when a sailor arrived with tall glasses in which we were served a mixture of tea and whisky, precisely what was needed to take the chill out of our bones. Convinced that within a few hours' time we would disembark on British soil, we raised our glasses in a heartfelt toast to Mother England. [2]

Unbeknownst to the new arrivals, instead of heading directly to the English coast, the submarine continued its routine patrol for another three days. The commander strongly advised his passengers to spend as much time as possible in their bunknowns and enjoy some well deserved rest. In reality, the last thing he wanted was to have the newcomers wandering aimlessly about his vessel creating possible disruptions for crew members who were concentrating on carrying out their assigned duties. In addition, he was well aware of the fact that stationary men use up less oxygen than those who are moving about.

These unexpected three days spent in the submarine's unfamiliar heat and humidity were remarkably difficult for me to endure. The uncomfortable and claustrophobic sensation of being helplessly confined only added to my consternation. The only saving grace was an invitation to take our meals with the commander. In fact, this entire underwater experience remains one of my least treasured wartime memories.

As it turned out, shortly before the end of our 'cruise,' the discomfort of being confined in cramped quarters was dramatically compounded by an unforeseen incident. Our first awareness of anything unusual was the alarming sound of propellers indicating the passage of another ship on the surface almost directly above us. A general alert was sounded, and hard on its heels, the order for a precipitous descent to a depth of about three hundred feet from the ocean floor. All engines were then stopped and absolute silence prevailed.

The vessel on the surface completed one long pass over our position; followed by a second passage, then two more. On the fifth pass, she launched some depth charges which mercifully detonated some distance from their mark. We did, however, sustain minor damage and were altogether rather badly shaken up. Light bulbs exploded and a few alarming leaks sprang up, but to our great relief, skilful crew members were able to repair them and relative calm was restored. As a precaution, we remained immobile and silent in the depths for two more hours before putting in at a safe harbour.

The extent of my fear during this episode of helpless entrapment knew no bounds—to the point where I became convinced that this was, in fact, my final ordeal. No words can express the rapture and relief that overcame me when I realized that I was actually going to get out of this sardine tin and find myself once again safe and sound, on terra firma.[3]

Along with one of his compatriots, who—like De La Rochefoucauld—was also more than a little shaken by the events of their prolonged Channel passage, the two were immediately welcomed into the waiting arms of the SOE.

Following precisely the same routine that he had experienced prior to his induction into the SOE, De La Rochefoucauld was sent off to the same camp outside London for a brief period of 'quarantine'. As a matter of course, there were questions to be answered relating to his extended stay in Paris following his successful escape. It was also necessary to ensure that he hadn't been 'turned' by the Gestapo while in their custody. It was a particularly legitimate concern at this point, due to a recent upheaval in the Gironde region of France.

One of the leaders of the "Scientist" Resistance network in the southwest of France, André Grandclément, had been 'turned' by the Germans with devastating results. As a consequence of this betrayal, the decision was reached that Grandclément and his wife must be 'neutralized' and the SOE transmitted orders to that effect.

Evidently, Friedrich Dohse, the head of the Gestapo in Bordeaux, had arrested Grandclément along with his wife and almost all of his Resistance network. In his dealings with Grandclément, Dohse's devious tactics proved all too persuasive. "We Germans may have lost the war; but after us, you will have the Communists. Show us the locations of your caches of weapons and I will free you and all your friends."

Grandclément may well have agonized over the decision, but in the end he capitulated and accepted Dohse's proposal with the result that several dozens of 'turned' Resistance members successfully infiltrated the Bordeaux region. With the network seriously compromised, the situation created by this act of betrayal was nothing short of a disaster.[4]

Meanwhile back in England, the de-briefing period for De La Rochefoucauld was predictably brief and he was given a clean bill of health in terms of future service in Churchill's secret army.

> I was then sent on to the same camp where I had originally undergone special ops training and was pleased to discover that some of the same instructors whom I had met over a year earlier were still passing on their finely-honed skills. My

sudden appearance on the scene created something of a stir as they had been convinced that having been captured, they were certain that I could not possibly have escaped the firing squad and had written me off as yet another loss. For them, I might just as well have returned from the Dead and hence the welcome I received from them was doubly warm. That first evening in March 1944, back among familiar faces with the whisky flowing freely, I was feeling very much alive and ready for whatever came my way.

For a few days I was treated to 'the good life' with plenty of rest and abundant food. Speculation was rife about an impending Allied landing, but no one seemed any the wiser about where or when it might take place. We were given to understand that crucial decisions had yet to be made. Finally, along with two other Frenchmen, I was summoned to the camp commander's office: it looked as if a new assignment could well be in the offing.

The commander confirmed that the invasion was imminent, but gave no hint of the time or place. Our objective would be to substantially weaken the enemy's resources destined for use against the anticipated Allied offensive. The mission was to be accomplished by organizing and carrying out the destruction of a major reserve of ammunition which the Germans had stockpiled in a factory close to Bordeaux near Saint-Ménard-en-Jalles.

Members of the local Resistance would be in place to assist with the completion of the operation. Those responsible for the orchestration of our mission had deemed it advisable for us—as trained experts in the use of explosives—to be

dropped by parachute into the vicinity.It went without saying that a mission of this kind could only be assigned to those
who expressed willingness to participate and it was quite apparent that the three of us were destined to become on-the-
spot volunteers. No further questions.

Since the operation was scheduled for sometime in May, we
were left with roughly ten days to prepare ourselves mentally
and physically and to receive specific training in much the
same way as I had for my first mission. This time, however,
we took part in a number of exercises with explosives and
with the use of plastics in particular.[5]

Prior to his imminent departure for this vitally important mission in France, De La Rochefoucauld was able to spend a brief period in London and in his 2002 memoir, he reminiscences admiringly
about the city and its people. "In spite of the enormous hardships to
which Londoners had been subjected during the Blitz, in spite of the
incredibly harsh and difficult conditions which they had endured for
so long, their inherent ability to maintain a stiff upper lip and keep
smiling had seen them through the darkest days."

Now the hope that victory was close at hand dominated the atmosphere and the dashing young Frenchman and his friends were
among the first to benefit from this spirit of renewed optimism. "We
were invited into the best homes in London and the girls fell into our
arms!" The rest is left to our imagination.

11

SABOTAGE ON A GRAND SCALE

Prior to the Allied D-Day invasion on the Normandy beaches, a joint American OSS and SOE covert operation was about to be launched. The plan—dubbed Jedburgh—involved dropping well-equipped teams of uniformed commandos into France as part of an extensive operation[1] to work in conjunction with the French Resistance in conducting acts of sabotage. To this end, massive drops of explosives and arms were organized in addition to shortwave radio equipment.

Given the circumstances, however, the pre-D-Day mission involving De La Rochefoucauld and his companions appears to have had no connection whatever with the Jedburgh scheme. In retrospect, though, the success of the mission assigned to them could scarcely have been surpassed.

Painted matte black, Lysander aircraft were used almost
exclusively for infiltrating and extracting agents and downed
fliers from the field in enemy-occupied France. Due to its
short landing and takeoff capabilities, it was ideally suited for
these dangerous clandestine missions. Photo courtesy of the
Canadian Warplanes Heritage Museum.

By the beginning of May, the 'volunteers' were back in top operational form, and were summoned once again to the commander's office for a final briefing. Here they were informed that the code name
of the operation was 'Soleil', and its objective was the destruction of
an armaments and munitions factory about twenty kilometres west
of Bordeaux on the road to Lacanau.

Maps of the region and plans of the factory building had been
provided in advance by the local Resistance network—the Bayard
group—which had also furnished valuable information regarding
the placement of the explosives and how to link them in such a way
that they would all blow up simultaneously. [2]

They were also informed that a few members of the Bayard réseau had actually managed to obtain employment as workmen in

the factory. Without question, with these infiltrators in place, their inside information could well prove more than useful to the would-be saboteurs.

At the end of the briefing we were told that the date for the drop was confirmed for 15 May.

Coincidentally, this was precisely the date scheduled for Eisenhower, Montgomery, and Churchill to discuss the soon-to-be implemented D-Day plans with His Majesty, King George VI.

Three of us—including a radio-operator—would be para-chuted in along with two containers, one packed with about two hundred pounds of explosives and the other filled with assorted weapons and ammunition.

On the evening of 14 May at a specially designated SOE airfield outside London, a plane was already on the tarmac awaiting our arrival. We boarded at the usual hour—around midnight—in order to be dropped at the site before daybreak. For some reason, the crew advised us to sleep a little while waiting for ' H hour', the time established for the parachute drop onto the appointed landing area—otherwise known as the DZ or Drop Zone. But during those few tense hours en route to our destination, the thought of dozing off was the furthest thing from our minds.

The flight itself was relatively uneventful, except for a few token anti-aircraft barrages fired at us by a watchful German artillery battery as we flew over the French coastline. Just before sunrise, the pilot took the customary pass over the drop zone and radio contact was established with the Bayard group, which had strategically positioned lights to facilitate the accuracy of the drop.

Then came the ritual of the great leap of faith into the unknown. The aircraft descended to five hundred feet—low enough that the parachutes were unlikely to be spotted as they floated to the ground. Red light—don't move. Green light—jump! One after another, we opened our chutes and were followed in short order by the two containers of explosives and armaments.

The drop zone was situated in a large clearing in the midst of a pine forest and my own landing went smoothly enough, however our wireless-operator was less fortunate and ended up with a badly sprained ankle. About ten men of the Bayard group had anxiously been awaiting our arrival and welcomed us with open arms. The chutes were gathered up and the containers moved with all possible speed and precision, while at the same time great care was taken to thoroughly erase all traces of our presence from the scene.

Following the customary routine, we rode off on bicycles; while the containers and our hapless radio-operator were stashed in a trailer and pulled along behind some of the cyclists. After pedalling for several miles in the dark, we arrived at one of the hidden locations which had been set up by the Bayard group. Here, we huddled together companionably in a small space under a rock face, skillfully camouflaged by some brushwood which rendered us invisible from prying eyes.[3]

Once safely hidden away, the new arrivals made the acquaintance of the renowned "Bayard"[4] who proved to be a most gracious host and opened a bottle of excellent Bordeaux in honour of the new-arrivals. Toasts were offered all around and a spirit of true bonhomie established, but before long, most of the 'welcoming committee' headed off on their bicycles, leaving the parachutists to catch up on their sleep. Undoubtedly the effects of the wine also helped to knit up the ravelled sleeve of care for the next few hours.

Later in the day, they formed up once again with Bayard and some of his lieutenants and he confirmed that in anticipation of 'Operation Soleil', in order to collect information vital to the success of the mission, three men of his group had been hired on by the unsuspecting German administration at the explosives factory along with about sixty other regular workers. In fact, these three men would be coming to meet with the group that same evening, after the factory closing hour at seven.

In the course of protracted discussions about how best to orchestrate the mission, De La Rochefoucauld put forward the idea that he should replace one of the three 'insiders' working at the plant, in order to personally place the explosives, link them together, and set them off at exactly the right moment once all the workers had left for the day.

At about half-past eight that evening, the three factory 'plants' arrived and together they began to work out the ultimate plan of action and the details for its implementation. They re-examined the layout of the factory down to the last inch and carefully pinpointed the exact placement of the explosives, munitions, and accelerants. The greatest challenge would be to decide upon the surest possible means of getting the required amount of putty-like green plastique[4] and the delayed fuses into the factory undetected. Finally, they would have to decide on the precise moment for igniting the fuse. And all of this would have to be accomplished within the allotted time. As usual, the devil was in the details. De La Rochefoucauld recalled:

As for the selection of the man whom I would be replacing, among the three conspirators employed at the factory, a young worker by the name of Pierre proved to be the ideal choice. He was about the same height, and—like me—had close-cropped hair. He wore dark glasses habitually, which, in itself, was an added and unforeseen advantage. And in the end it was unanimously agreed that for the purposes of infiltration into the plant, Pierre was the man I would replace.

Pierre then handed me his identity card and papers, but—of necessity—the photo would have to be substituted with my own. To complete the impersonation, I would, of course, wear his dark glasses and coveralls. The few kilos of plastique and the accessories we required for the operation would be carefully inserted into baguettes identical in every way to those the other workers brought to work for lunch each day. The remaining items would be then be concealed in the heels of shoes especially modified for this purpose.

Since it was already Saturday, it was decided that we would begin setting up for the operation the following Monday and by Thursday evening—once the workers had left at seven— everything should be in place for the fireworks. It would then be up to me to remain in the factory to set off the explosives while, at the same time, taking the extra precaution of a setting a delayed fuse which would leave a twenty minute 'window' for me to make my exit.

We made efficient use of Sunday to get our materials under secure cover and to pack the plastic explosives into the baguettes. It was necessary to take great pains in slicing open each of these, as the crust of those fresh loaves has a tendency to flake and tear. This operation required infinite patience and a sharp serrated blade in order to hollow out the soft interior and replace it with the 'paté plastique'. As a result, the conspirators' mid-day meal would be reduced to the outside crust, which, in any event, has traditionally had the benefit of being considered the best part of any baguette.

Having acquired from Pierre virtually all the items necessary to allow me to impersonate him without being recognized, we parted company until the following morning when we would rendez-vous outside the factory to begin our own essential work towards the war effort.[5]

Thursday morning, accompanied by Bayard, De La Rochefoucauld arrived on his bicycle at the factory, where he met his two new 'colleagues' who were already there among the crowd of workers a good fifteen minutes before the start of the work day. At 8 o'clock sharp, the plant door opened and with it the first real frisson of fear. Would he make it through the routine inspection for entry? This could well be the most crucial hurdle—the moment when the success or failure of the entire mission hung in the balance.

In single file and at a snail's pace, with lunch bags slung across their shoulders, the men shuffled slowly towards the German soldier responsible for checking each worker's identity papers. It was essential, of course, that De La Rochefoucauld maintain an air of casual nonchalance as he inched forward towards the guard. As luck would have it, this particular functionary was somewhat less than attentive to his duties and made only a cursory check of the workers' cards before permitting them to enter the premises. No inspection of the contents of the lunch bags or footwear. Nothing further. In

the highly-touted efficiency department of Germany's military ma-
chinery, this was one member of the Master Race who had clearly let
down the side. A slacker.

Stage One having now been successfully completed, it was on to
the next. Once inside the building, along with a few other workers,
"Pierre of the Dark Glasses" was assigned to unloading crates from
a convoy of trucks which had come in the night before. The crates
were then to be hauled in to the factory itself on the other side of a
courtyard. What better way to become familiarised with the general
lay of the land and to take one's bearings among the different buildings, as well as to pinpoint the location of the fuel depot?

It is one thing to carefully scrutinize plans drawn up on paper
and often quite another to be in a position to physically assess their
accuracy. In this case, however, the two matched up with such precision, that our man of the hour had the distinct impression he had
worked in this factory for years and knew every square inch of its
layout. An old hand with a few new tricks…

While in the process of doing the rounds, I was also able to
note some important and useful points. I ascertained, for example, that factory guard duty—no doubt considered by the
Germans to be something less than strenuous or life-threat-
ening—had been assigned to older soldiers, who paid us
virtually no attention, as they chatted and joked among
themselves to while away the hours. Capitalizing on these
fortuitous circumstances, we managed—between Monday
and Thursday—to successfully place about forty kilograms
of plastic explosives in the various locations we had selected
beforehand—including the fuel depot.

What's more, I had been able to map out my own escape route
after accomplishing my mission. Since the door to the plant

was locked directly after the workers' departure, I had to select a suitable place to avoid detection. With this in mind, I
made a mental note of a small dormer window, with a number of crates piled beneath it. Better still, it opened onto a
courtyard and the twenty-foot perimeter wall that I would
have to scale to make my escape. It was agreed that Bayard
and his men would wait on the other side at this particular
spot and would toss a rope over the wall to help me get up
and over and out of harm's way. They would, of necessity, also
be on full alert, with weapons at the ready in the event that an
enemy patrol should appear on the scene.

There was, however, a slight problem in that I had not been
able to link the charges which would blow up the factory
and those placed at the fuel depot located a hundred yards
away. The solution I hit upon was to stagger the triggering of
the delayed fuses. By this method, the detonators at the fuel
depot would be activated at 6:30 with a delay of one hour,
and those at the actual factory would be set for 7:00—quit-
ting time for the workers—with a delay of thirty minutes.
The entire shooting match was therefore programmed to
begin at 7:30. Zero Hour!

On Day 'J' for Jeudi (Thursday), the hours passed without
incident, although admittedly we were very much on edge.
I placed the last charges in the factory and linked them up.
Then at about 18:30, I put the detonators in place, and found
a way to approach the fuel depot without arousing undue attention when the time came for me to ignite the detonator.
Having accomplished this, I re-entered the factory, praying
to the Almighty that the detonators would both work, and
most of all, that they would work at the specified times.

From my pre-selected hiding place I was able to observe two German soldiers doing the rounds of the building. After what seemed like an eternity, they finally made their exit and locked the doors behind them. At seven o'clock sharp, I heard the siren which signalled the departure of the workers.

The moment had come to ignite the delayed detonators in the factory building which were to set off the explosion thirty minutes later. Once that was accomplished, I clambered up the pile of crates, cleared access to the dormer window, broke the panes as quietly as possible, hurtled down into the court-yard, and dashed towards the perimeter wall. I had barely reached the base of it, when two ropes tossed down from outside landed on my head. Never in my life, either before or since, have I scaled a twenty-foot wall any faster. On the other side, I fell straight into Bayard's waiting arms.

The bicycles were in place and within seconds we were ped-alling at top speed to get clear of the vicinity and make for our cachette located only a mile or so from the scene of the crime. But before long curiosity got the better of us and we stopped to listen—counting the seconds as we strained our ears in anticipation. Then we heard it—the first earth-shak-ing blast followed in short order by a second explosion that seemed to shake the sky itself. Operation Soleil had been a success! Mission accomplished.[6]

But this was neither the time nor the place to linger, so once again they took to their bicycles in all possible haste and made for the appointed hiding place. Here, at long last they could catch their breath and begin to relax. The pressure and apprehension of the past four days had taken its toll however, and De La Rochefoucauld recalls feeling close to immobilized by stress and fatigue.

Bayard, however, had other plans. Based on the assumption that De La Rochefoucauld would return safely from the mission, Bayard had laid on a copious celebratory feast accompanied by several bottles of excellent wine—all of which proved highly restorative until sleep deprivation and exhaustion took their toll.

But first a message must be transmitted to London to report the successful outcome of all those carefully laid plans. De La Rochefoucauld and the radio-operator put their heads together and composed the message. Still recovering from the effects of his injury during the drop, the radioman was barely capable of walking, however his more essential skills remained otherwise unimpaired and he quickly established contact. The message transmitted was appropriately understated and to the point: "Operation Soleil successful." The response received went one better and consisted of a single word: "Congratulations!"

As the celebration wound down, the other co-conspirators made their farewells and rode off into the night to rejoin their wives and families. This left only Bayard, the radio-operator and one totally exhausted escape artist who collapsed onto a bed of straw and was instantly dead to the world. Tomorrow would take care of itself.

After a good ten hours' sleep, aside from the minimal after-effects of the wine from the night before, all three woke up in good form. Because the ill-fated radio-operator was unable to do more than hobble a few steps, it was decided that he should remain with the Bayard group which would do its utmost to keep him out of harm's way until he was fit for repatriation.

As for De La Rochefoucauld—two more days' rest were in order before he was ready to set off on his bicycle for a rendezvous in Bordeaux. Here he was scheduled to meet with a special contact who would be in a position to arrange for him to be smuggled back to England. In any case, it seemed better to err on the side of caution and wait for a reasonable amount of time to elapse in the hope that the upheaval over the demolition of the explosives plant at Saint-Médard-en-Jalles might have subsided.

Inevitably, the entire area would have been immediately placed under concentrated surveillance by German patrols, however, with any luck, De La Rochefoucauld's little excursion in the dark—and well after curfew—might be somewhat less risky after a few days' delay.

News that the atmosphere in Bordeaux had begun to change for the better only served to bolster the young Frenchman's spirits. The Germans had evidently become increasingly demoralized by local events which included several attempted assassinations. As a precautionary measure, they had begun confining themselves to moving about in columns and it was becoming more and more evident that their presence and control in the city was beginning to diminish. On the other hand, the fact that they continued to be in command of the entire region represented a threat that could not be overlooked.

Just after nightfall on Saturday 22 May, I bade a fond farewell to Bayard and my radio-operator, jumped on my bicycle, and without any lights, started off for Bordeaux using only the back roads where at that time of night there was virtually no traffic, Even at that, not once but twice, I heard the sound of a motor in the distance. Taking no chances, I braked instantly, flung my bike into the ditch, and crouched down instinctively. Nothing!

Once the coast was apparently clear, I hauled my bike back onto the road and with some trepidation pedalled on towards Bordeaux. Just a few more miles and I would be at the safe house. Twice I had managed to avoid detection. The question was, would my luck hold out a third time?

The answer was upon me almost before I knew it. On a curve, a barrier had been set up between two farm buildings and I barely had time to brake to avoid smashing directly into the barricade. Two German soldiers appeared out of nowhere, lights full on, machine guns ready to open fire on a moment's notice. My only alternative was to raise my arms, doing my utmost not to appear panic-stricken. In barely intelligible French, I was asked whether I had a permit to be out at night after curfew. Where was the proverbial 'Ausweis' or identity papers that I should have in my possession at all times?

Regrettably I was unable to produce one, but made a valiant attempt at a plausible explanation. "I was just returning home after making love with my girlfriend in the woods," I responded with a sheepish grin, however my charade failed to impress my captors, who clearly had no sense of romance. In short order, I had been shoved into a truck and was on my way to Bordeaux. Then, almost before I knew what was happening, the doors of the dreaded Fort Hâ prison had slammed shut behind me.[7]

12 CAPTORS FOILED AGAIN

On that Sunday morning at dawn, barely ten days had passed since De La Rochefoucauld and his radio operator had been parachuted in to La Gironde region to set the wheels of Operation Soleil in motion. And yet here he was—once again—at the mercy of the enemy. The worst imaginable fate! There was always the faint hope, of course, that they might find his affaire du coeur explanation for being on the road in the small hours of the morning almost believable. He was, after all, a Frenchman, however, given the rising tide of apprehension over an imminent Allied invasion, realistically, the chances of this were next to nil.

Having passed through the gates of the sombre Fortress du Hâ[1] which was home at that time to a thousand other 'political detainees', he was marched off to the reception desk, where a non-commissioned officer and two regulars were on hand to process new arrivals.

Not surprisingly, his desperate attempt to explain to the officer in charge that he had been apprehended in error elicited nothing more than a derogatory sneer of derision accompanied by the inevitable advice that he should hang on to his explanations and present them to the prosecuting judge. In the meantime, the prisoner was to be escorted to cool his heels in a nearby detention room.

Somehow, this disastrous turn of events must have seemed all the more devastating falling as it did so hard on the heels of the exhilarating success of *Operation Soleil*....

I had precisely a day and a night to reflect on the possible explanations which I, Rene Lallier, could present to the judge, but I was already well aware that this was little more than an exercise in futility. In reality, there wasn't even the faintest glimmer of hope that I was going to be able to respond appropriately to any of the questions that might be put to me.

Had I any information to offer about the identity and whereabouts of my mythical paramour? No... Could I provide the name of the person whom I was on my way to visit in Bordeaux? No, once again, as this would be tantamount to a betrayal of my contact there. What's more, the prosecutor would undoubtedly have already succeeded in making the fairly obvious connection between the pathetic vagabond standing in the prisoner's dock and the recent fireworks at nearby Saint-Médard-en-Jalles.

In short—to all intents and purposes—my situation was hopeless, Utterly hopeless. Only two solutions presented themselves to me and the first was far from appealing. Any inclination I might have had to end my life by ingesting the little pill that had been carefully concealed in the heel of one of my shoes was immediately set aside. I knew with absolute certainty that I was not yet prepared to die, so this last-ditch means of ending it all would definitely remain in its hiding place for a time when truly desperate measures were called for.[2]

In a retrospective flash, it also came back to me that—for reasons unrevealed—a cyanide pill had not been on the list of necessities for my first mission near Avallon. Almost certainly the inclusion of the lethal pill on this occasion indicated that my British controllers considered my recent mission in the Gironde to be sufficiently hazardous to warrant issuing me with the means to take my own life. Under the circumstances, the chances of being taken prisoner and held for interrogation were far from remote.[3]

My second alternative—which at that moment appeared close to insurmountable—was to make an attempt at escape. Having already accomplished this successfully at Auxerre by making a run for it after leaping off the back of the truck en route to my execution, there was always the chance that a second miracle might just be waiting to happen.

Applying a dose of practical logic to the situation, it seemed clear that—come what may—an attempt at escape was a far more appealing option than cyanide. Now, during the course of the remaining fateful hours, all I needed was to apply all my powers of imagination and ingenuity to come up with a workable plan. And should it fail, I could always fall back on the first and final solution—my little death-dealing pill.[4]

After desperately wracking his brain, the captive suddenly remembered that while he was being held for questioning a year earlier in the prison at Auxerre, his cellmate had had an epileptic seizure. De La Rochefoucauld had immediately called out to the guard who arrived to investigate and had helped to lift his stricken companion onto his bunk. The guard had then made off in search of a doctor.

In the dire situation in which he now found himself, it occurred to De La Rochefoucauld that he might just make use of this past experience by creating a similar scenario. In any case, it was certainly worth making an attempt. Nothing ventured. Nothing gained.

Sometime during the night between Sunday and Monday, he would simulate a seizure of his own. Thanks to his well-developed powers of observation, he had noticed on his arrival at Fort du Hâ in the small hours of Sunday morning that only three guards had been on duty in the front office.

The halfway mark of the 'graveyard shift 'seemed an ideal time to put his plan into action. Towards two o'clock in the morning—having somehow broken off the leg of a piece of furniture in the room in which he was being held—he stretched out on the floor, and set his simulated seizure into motion. Feverishly writhing about in all directions, screaming and screeching like a banshee to attract the guards' attention, mere moments passed before he detected the reassuring click of the observation peephole in the door. Spurred on by the knowledge that his actions had prompted an immediate response, he increased the intensity of his contortions.

Armed with his makeshift cudgel, he watched anxiously as the key turned in the lock and the door opened. With lightning speed, he was instantly on his feet and had hurled himself at the guard who stood framed in the doorway. Using the leg of furniture to strike with full force on the back of the fellow's head, he then proceeded to twist his neck in a precise and effective duplication of the tactic he had learned from his British instructors.

But this was scarcely the moment for indulging in self-congratulation. Having assured himself that the unsuspecting guard had been effectively dispatched, the would-be escapee hastily donned his victim's jacket, pocketed his keys, and removed the safety catch on his gun as he made for the outer reception area. Here, as foreseen, sat two sleepy and unsuspecting German guards slumped in their chairs. Fortunately the lighting in the room was dim enough that they were both temporarily deceived by the jacket of their comrade's uniform and failed to register that the man entering the room was anything but a compatriot.

I approached and fired point-blank at the first guard, who instantly slumped over just as the second one made a vain attempt to spring into action. Too little, too late ! Before he even had time to draw his weapon, I had gunned him down as well. Had it not been for those intense and rigorous training sessions I had been subjected to back in England, it is difficult to imagine that—at twenty-one years of age—in the space of two minutes, I had just killed three men! And I was not even out of the building…

The key to the exit door was in the lock and I decided it would be a charitable act to help myself to all the other keys while I was at it. After opening the door that led out into the dark streets, before taking off, I locked all the other doors for good measure. Later the keys were pitched into the first drain hole I came upon. At this point, I was still wearing the uniform jacket belonging to my guard and was armed with his gun. My first priority, of course, was to locate my contact without further delay.

After a while I decided to stop running, and slowly, deliberately, I caught my breath and proceeded to make my way calmly but cautiously across the deserted and silent city of Bordeaux. Fortunately I had earlier committed to memory in precise detail a map of the city, and this enabled me—without too much difficulty—to locate my contact's home on a modest little street towards the outskirts of town. It turned out to be a small house with an enclosed front garden and an iron gate which had been locked from the inside. After climbing over this without difficulty, I was able to approach the house and knock on the front door with a hopeful heart.

After a moment or two, a second storey window flew open and a man in pyjamas peered out wanting to know who the devil was pounding on his door in the middle of the night.

I called up to him in a stage whisper, "It's me. René Lallier. You were expecting me on Saturday night but I got held up."

"Good Lord"! he exclaimed. "I'll be right down."

The door was flung open and almost instantly I felt the urge to laugh uproariously. The look on my host's face was beyond compare. He stood as if he were rooted to the floor—completely and utterly aghast at the sight of me standing in his hallway wearing the uniform jacket I had 'borrowed' from the German guard. And once I had regaled him with the rest of the story and where I had spent the past twenty-four hours, he was left utterly aghast. It was certainly not every day that a prisoner managed to break out of Fort Hâ let alone live to tell the tale.

My associate was also able to pass on to me the news that the sabotage of the explosives factory at Saint-Médard-en-Jalles—attributed by the press to the Communists—[5] had created an enormous furor. No doubt news of my escape would only help to rekindle the excitement. Taking the jacket which had been so instrumental in the success of my escape, my new-found friend rolled it up into a ball and assured me of his intention to dispose of this incriminating piece of evidence at the earliest opportunity.

My gracious host's next priority was to put together something for us to eat accompanied—as always—by a good bottle of restorative wine, which was no doubt every bit as rewarding for him as it was for me. Within minutes of savouring the last drop of wine, I was sound asleep. Once again, tomorrow was left to take care of itself.[6]

A few hours' sleep was all that was required to put the newly escaped De La Rochefoucauld back in good form, but the difficulties facing him and his host the next morning were not quite so easily resolved. With the help of his contact, whose nom de guerre was Jean, De La Rochefoucauld decided to attempt to make contact with 'Aristide', an important SOE strategist who was not a stranger to him as they already knew one another from having met in England. Aristide had actually been the instigator of the operation at Saint-Médard-en-Jalles and lived in Bordeaux with his wife who was a native of the city.[7]

Aristide's role was to supervise the parachute drops of weapons, as well as to hide and evacuate agents who had been sent from England on missions to the Bordeaux area. As he had been waiting to hear from De La Rochefoucauld since the preceding Saturday evening, it seemed a matter of some urgency to advise Aristide of the intervening events—an arrest, three dead German soldiers and a successful escape.

However, Jean's response to making contact erred on the side of caution. "I'm going to go and see Aristide first and alert him to the situation. In the meantime, you remain here and rest up. You'll find lots of good suspense novels in the library. Mind you, these stories are a lot less extraordinary than yours, but at least they'll provide you with a bit of distraction while I'm gone."

Over and above his activities with the Resistance, Jean held an identity card entitling him to work as a travelling salesman peddling kitchenware. This allowed him to move freely around Bordeaux all day long, so he set off with his case of catalogues, warning his visitor not to expect him back until just before curfew.

"I've had quite a day," he announced on his return. "The entire city is in an uproar with police everywhere. I was asked twice to show my papers. However, I did manage to see Aristide and he advised me to keep you under wraps for a while longer to let things simmer down. He will arrange to see you next Thursday afternoon."

Circumstance was offering me three days' relaxation. Three days to indulge in sleep, to read and to eat as much as I wanted, while Jean was out from morning till night. In the evenings, we discussed what I should do to avoid control points and searches and how best to disguise myself when I left the house to go to meet with Aristide. After reviewing the situation several times, Jean suddenly hit upon an ingenious possibility.

His sister, having taken her vows and entered a convent, had left behind a complete made-to-measure nun's habit and—as luck would have it—she also happened to be considerably taller than the average Frenchwoman. So I tried on the robe— actually a bit short in the leg—but the veil and headdress fit perfectly, and the black stockings covered up my legs. In fact, the whole outfit, including the indispensable rosary, looked quite convincing. Then came the final touches. Some make-up base and a generous application of face powder produced the desired effect. And so it was that this altogether happy co-incidence worked exceedingly well in my favour, as I would be able to move freely about the city without being remotely obvious. An entirely innocent-looking nun on the run!

We then carefully laid out various other details of my Thursday excursion into town including our route to Aristide's house. Jean would walk some distance ahead of me and I would follow in his wake. When he reached our destination, he would indicate this by giving a pre-arranged signal, then continue walking, leaving me to enter alone.

We started off towards the end of the day, with Jean in the lead and I following about a hundred metres behind him. I had asked him to walk at a moderate pace; and this was just as well because, as we made our way to our destination, I was finding it difficult not to get tripped up by my unaccustomed garb. Advancing in a rather sedate fashion, it took us at least an hour to reach our destination on a small street. Jean hesitated for an instant in front of one of the houses, glanced at it, then continued walking. According to plan, I went up to the door and proceeded to ring the doorbell. Almost at once a woman opened the door and inquired about the nature of my visit.

"I would like to speak with Monsieur Aristide," I murmured.

"Come in, Sister, come in… I am Madame Aristide and I'm the one in this household who looks after charitable donations."

"But I would like to speak personally with Mr. Aristide," I insisted resolutely.

"Very well. I shall go and inform him, then" she replied, obviously slightly perplexed. "Would you please be good enough to wait here for a few minutes?"

At that, Madame Aristide turned and disappeared into the interior of the house, shrugging her shoulders, and no doubt asking herself what this strange nun could possibly want from her husband. Meanwhile I decided to further refine my role as a pillar of earthly virtue by seating myself discreetly in a contemplative pose; my legs pressed closely together and my hands clasped in my sleeves.

A few minutes later, a door opened and Aristide appeared looking puzzled and without the faintest sign of recognition.

"How may I help you, Sister? he inquired uncertainly.

At this point it was impossible for me to contain myself any longer. I stood up, went over to him, and gave him a hearty slap on the back.

"You don't recognize me? It's me—Lallier. And you were supposed to be expecting me today."

"What in the name of God! I don't believe it! No one warned me about any disguise. When my wife told me that there was a very persistent nun at the door who insisted on seeing me in person, I was convinced she was bringing me a message that something disastrous had happened to you." [8]

The two then burst into gales of laughter and La Rochfoucauld started in on his tale of madcap misadventure and escape, while intermittently exchanging more slaps on the back, as if to reassure themselves that they were actually both there—alive and kicking. Hearing the male voices and the ensuing commotion, Madame Aristide returned to the room, her face a study at the sight of her husband in the arms of the mysterious nun.

Aristide immediately dispelled any misunderstanding by introducing Lallier, and explaining that this was, indeed, the young man he had been expecting, although certainly not in this pious incarnation! With a hearty laugh, Madame Aristide also embraced the good sister proving once again that laughter and danger often walk hand in hand.

Following this warm welcome chez Aristide, thoughts of putting together plans to arrange for his return to England were next on the agenda. This, however, turned out to be easier said than done, and—in the end—it was not until well after Germany had surrendered in early May of the following year that De La Rochefoucauld was briefly reunited in London with his surviving confreres from the SOE.

For the moment, his orders were to remain in hiding and await further contact. What he did not know was that the combined Allied forces were within a matter of days of launching *Operation Overlord*—the long-awaited D-Day invasion on the beaches of Normandy.[9] On high alert, SOE headquarters was understandably preoccupied with finalizing its part in the last-minute details of this historic landing. At this moment, the repatriation of an operative to England—and a Frenchman at that—was most likely the very least of their worries.

And so it was arranged that, in the interval, De La Rochefoucauld would be passed on to a certain Monsieur Demont, a member of the Resistance movement who was also operating a legitimate business in the southwest of France's Landes region, just to the south of Bordeaux. At the behest of Aristide, M. Demont was evidently prepared to offer employment to a certain young Frenchman as a labourer in his operation.

By the end of the month of May—accompanied by Aristide—
SOE agent, Robert De La Rochefoucauld, still bearing the identity papers of the elusive René Lallier, was en route to meet his new
employer who specialised in the production of wooden supporting
beams for the mining industry.

Both men were received by M. Demont with great hospitality,
but it quickly became clear that even with this trusted comrade,
Aristide was exercising extreme caution. De La Rochefoucauld was
introduced not as a fugitive from the Gestapo but simply a young
Frenchman desperate to avoid the possibility of being shipped off
as part of the compulsory work force destined to contribute to
Germany's war effort [10] Then, within ten days of his arrival chez
Demont, came the long-awaited news of the successful Allied landing in Normandy.

General de Gaulle's subsequent call to arms was immediately extended to all patriotic Frenchmen throughout the country and in particular to those already active in the Resistance movement—hence-
forth to be known as the F.F.I. or French Forces of the Interior. At the
time of the D-Day invasion, de Gaulle is said to have estimated that
France's Resistance strength stood at roughly one hundred thousand.

After four long years of German occupation, those who had
fought so courageously in the shadows had been aching for the day
to arrive when they could come out into the open against their oppressors. Many threw caution to the wind and opted to wear the red,
white and blue brassards or armbands which were widely distributed
along with weapons and ammunition. The armbands also bore the
initials F.F.I. and the emblem of the Cross of Lorraine.

Those who chose to wear these brassards were not, however,
guaranteed any protection whatever under the terms of the Geneva
Convention, as they were never officially designated as uniformed soldiers in the accepted sense. If apprehended by the Germans, who appeared disinclined to beat a hasty retreat to the Fatherland, they would

be summarily shot as civilians bearing arms. By openly displaying the armband, they were also setting themselves up as targets for betrayal—a fate which sadly awaited more than a few of these zealous patriots.

The Resistance movement, as a whole, had been well prepared for its part in the weeks and months following the Allied landing. As if on cue, telephone wires and cables were cut, roads and railway lines rendered impassable, bridges blown and power plants destroyed. In short, an unparalleled degree of chaos was visited on the German occupying forces across the length and breadth of France. On the other hand, these successes were offset by the brutality of German reprisals. In one horrendous instance, six hundred women and children were burned alive in a village church by the infamous S.S. Division, *Das Reich*. In other parts of the country, executions of fifty or sixty hostages were not uncommon. And all these atrocities perpetrated in the name of the Almighty Führer![11]

Robert De La Rochefoucauld captured on camera wearing the uniform of the French Forces of the Interior, June 1944. Courtesy the De La Rochefoucauld family archives.

13 VIVE LA FRANCE

On the morning of 25 August, 1944 an enormous crowd of jubilant Parisians welcomed the arrival of the 2nd French Armored Division led by General Philippe Leclerc de Hauteclocque, which had successfully occupied the western part of Paris, including the Arc de Triomphe and the Champs Elysées. For their part, American troops had cleared the eastern sector of the city and received an equally memorable welcome while in the course of the previous night, the main German Occupying Force had almost entirely evacuated the city.

Galvanized by the knowledge that at long last there were French troops on the ground in France, De La Rochefoucauld was impatient to be doing something more useful than transporting mine timbers. To add to his frustration, he had received no further word from his British controllers. The enticing possibility of leaving the relative safety of his employment with Mr. Demont became more tempting by the day. In the end, he took steps to join a local Resistance group by contacting its maquisard leader, Léonce Dussarat, known as "The Lion of the Landes", who had evidently been charged with orchestrating the liberation of Bordeaux.

General Philippe Leclerc,
Commander of France's
Second Division and celebrated
liberator of Paris, 19 August,
1944. Photo courtesy of the
Musée Leclerc, Paris.

With one dramatic exception, the brief period that I spent
with Dussarat and his companions was not particularly active. My most vivid memory of those few weeks with this
Resistance group involves an incident which had the distinction of proving once and for all that I was indeed blessed
with that often elusive attribute so vital to those engaged in
subversive activities. Pure unadulterated luck!

With my group leader and another member of our réseaux,
we were en route to meet with the leader of a second group of
maquis, when, without warning, a German patrol appeared
out of nowhere. One of us succeeded in eluding pursuit,
however my group leader and I were taken prisoner on the
spot and immediately transported to a nearby village which,

by coincidence, was the site of the local German Command Post—a quasi-headquarters manned by about ten soldiers.

We were marched into in a room on the main floor facing the street and our interrogation began almost at once, however the combination of the Germans' fractured French and our dramatic pretense at failing to understand their questions temporarily contained the situation. Suddenly, we heard an automobile drawing to a halt directly in front of the building. Perhaps the Gestapo had come to join us?

Through the window, we were able to catch a quick glimpse of three men emerging from the vehicle, submachine guns in hand. Seconds later, they had begun spraying the room where we were being held. Without a moment's hesitation, I flattened myself under a table, and dragged our group leader down with me. At that moment, it seemed that the worst danger facing us was the distinct possibility that we would be gunned down by our own friendly fire.

With bullets whining all around us, I began shouting at the top of my voice that we were on the same side, but it was all completely in vain. The bullets kept on coming, so I decided to switch tactics. "We surrender! We surrender!" I called out and still the hail of bullets continued unabated. Finally, to my undying relief, the attack ended in our favour and within a few minutes, we were being trundled into the rescue vehicle and driven swiftly off to the relative safety of the countryside.

Our dramatic rescue and newfound freedom was, of course, all thanks to our third companion-at-arms, who had earlier succeeded in escaping capture by the German patrol. He had raced back at top speed to the base camp which was only a few kilometres from where we had been apprehended and reported to the group's second-in command that we had fallen into enemy hands. Together, they concluded that in all likelihood we would have been transported to the nearest enemy headquarters for questioning and together they immediately resolved to come and liberate us.

In retrospect, I admit to having been absolutely terror-stricken throughout the course of this entire incident. In fact, I was quite convinced that we were both going to die right then and there. But once again, Fate intervened and snatched me from the clutches of the Germans without so much as a scratch. And in this instance, I had even been shielded from French bullets into the bargain![1]

This incredible stroke of luck was followed by a period of relative doldrums. In August 1944, the local Resistance forces set out to mount an attack on Bordeaux with the intention of liberating the city only to discover that the Germans had already pulled out. Just a few months earlier, De La Rochefoucauld had walked these same streets and crossed the same squares noting that the German Occupation forces were still very much in evidence—to the point where the citizens of Bordeaux had become all but invisible.

In the days that followed the German evacuation, it seemed as if the entire French Army had invaded the city en masse. De La Rochefoucauld describes the almost oppressive presence of French militia in dress uniform enjoying an aperitif on the terraces of the cafés, while others in battle dress, with weapons at the ready, were patrolling the city with an excessive air of authority. The entire scenario struck him as unnecessarily overbearing. And this, in turn, became the source of a certain sense of disenchantment for the young agent provocateur, whose own training had prepared him to operate invisibly in the shadows.

At the Bordeaux harbour, the quays were deserted, the warehouses closed; and the docks empty. Not even a wisp of smoke to announce a ship's movement; no sailors in the Chartrons district. But how could it have been otherwise? The Germans were blockading the port by locking up the estuary to the north with a force of twenty-five thousand— fifteen thousand at Royan and ten thousand at Graves Point on the opposite bank. This was where the real action was taking place. It was time to move in that direction.

Although at that point, he was still operating with Léonce Dussarat and his group in the Landes, De La Rochefoucauld had come to the conclusion that they could participate more actively by aligning themselves with Charly group. This unit of the Resistance, which originated in Médoc had re-located itself in Saint-Laurent close to the frontline at Graves Point and was facing a concentration of ten thousand German troops who had dug in and appeared determined to hold their ground.

The newcomers to Charly group were welcomed with open arms by its commander Comminetti—alias Charly—who, at that point, was desperately short of men. Because of this, the activities of the group had necessarily been drastically limited. Their proximity to the Germans' heavily defended front line dictated that their most effective tactic involved instigating skirmishes on the periphery of the zone held by the Germans. The hope was that this would help to keep the enemy troops at bay.

On the other hand, because they were so drastically outnumbered, it was impossible for the Resistance fighters to advance further into enemy territory. Against the strategically positioned German pillboxes and heavy artillery, Charly group's few submachine guns and grenades were hopelessly and frustratingly inadequate.

At some point during this period of 'hit and run' warfare, an incident occurred which—for De La Rochefoucauld—exemplified the indiscriminate fortunes of war and its many absurdities.

We were carrying out a series of patrols along the German lines and in one instance I had occasion to push open the door of an empty building with my revolver held at the ready. At precisely the same moment, on the other side of the room, another door opened to reveal the silhouette of a German. Instinctively, I fired five rounds in his direction, while the reverse reaction on his part was sending a hail of bullets into mine. Then, just as if we had been participants in a well-orchestrated duel, each of us disappeared through his own doorway. Whether any of my bullets found their mark remains one of those unanswered questions that accumulate over time, however my own souvenir of the incident was limited to a few tell-tale holes in my cap.

It was also during this same period of activity with the Resistance in the Gironde, that I noticed the large numbers of Jews who had joined our ranks. On one occasion, in a casual conversation with a Jewish companion, I broached the subject with him. "No mystery there," came his reply. "We have had a very highly-placed contact working within the local Police Headquarters. He generally warns us whenever one of us is about to be arrested by the Germans or when a roundup has been planned. Then, rather than allow ourselves to be apprehended, we take to the woods." The Secretary-General of the police for the Bordeaux region at the time was Maurice Papon,[2] although it was not until many years later that I finally met the man in question.[3]

To a certain extent, the truth of the above remark concerning Papon's role may well have applied to certain Jews in this particular region, however, the tragic fact remains that from a total population of approximately 350,000 Jews, the vast majority of the 76,000 Jews deported from France between 1942 and 1944 died in Nazi extermination camps.

14 OPEN WARFARE

Then, in the late autumn of 1944, official orders were issued by veteran Free French General Larminat[1] to the effect that the Resistance forces were to be reconstituted to form what would become France's Third Army. And by December, Robert De La Rochefoucauld had been inducted as an officer in the newly-formed brigade of Free French forces for the Graves-Royan region. This change in status also marked a distinct turning point from a world of secrets and sabotage to that of straightforward soldiering and all that this entailed.

To prepare for a final attack on the heavily defended Graves Point, which lay on the estuary northwest of Bordeaux, French troops had been deployed to continue harassing the enemy at various points along the lines. It fell to the newly-minted young officer, De La Rochefoucauld, to prepare his men for these hit-and-run operations by introducing them to the basic commando tactics in much the same way as he had been trained for this type of combat in England three years earlier. A wealth of experience put to the best possible use.

Having long since become accustomed to adapting to whatever happened to come his way and making the best of it, the transition from the life of a Special Operations agent engaged in subversion and destruction to that of an officer in the French military appears to have come easily to De La Rochefoucauld. In his memoir, he describes an incident which reflects both his understated sense of humour and his obvious talent for making friends easily.

In February 1945, during a routine inspection, we received a visit from, General de Larminat, who requested that each of the officers in turn should introduce himself to the exalted commander-in-chief. So when the moment arrived, I saluted and presented myself accordingly:

"De La Rochefoucauld."

Larminat's response suggested that he was less than amused. "I asked you for your real name, not your nom de guerre".At which point I was forced to explain that my real name was, indeed, De La Rochefoucauld. To his credit, the General immediately burst out laughing. How could he possibly have known that I had long-since abandoned the pseudonym of Lallier? Nor could he have been apprised of the fact that a good number of my fellow-officers had been having a bit of good-natured fun at my expense by invoking the memory of my distinguished literary ancestor, the renowned seventeenth-century maximist, François De La Rochefoucauld.[2] Hence my recently acquired nickname "Maxime".[3]

By April 1945, nearly ten months after D-Day, most—if not all of France—had been liberated. On the Atlantic coast, however, there remained two isolated pockets on the Gironde Estuary, where the Germans were making a determined last stand. On April 15th, the decision was taken to launch an offensive in order to liberate these two locations. But in order to accomplish this, it would be necessary to substantially weaken the heavily fortified defenses of the enemy. Around the perimeter of the two bastions at Graves Point and Royan, the German Wehrmacht had constructed a large number of pillboxes and anti-tank traps. As well, behind the lines, they had stockpiled substantial quantities of food and munitions in heavily reinforced concrete blockhouses.

When the order came to attack, we were well aware that we could expect stiff resistance on the ground. To help to soften up this well-entrenched enemy force, it had been decided that the Allies would first launch a massive air attack. Their primary target was the anti-tank defenses in order to allow our vehicles to break through the perimeter. Next on the agenda was the destruction of the almost impregnable concrete blockhouses. It soon became clear that thus far the damage inflicted on these strongly reinforced structures had been minimal and our assault units were in for a tough battle to put them out of commission.

In the sector to which we had been assigned, not far from Saint-Vivien-du-Médoc and bordering the Gironde River, we were subjected to constant fire, coming mainly from a blockhouse which had been repeatedly bombed by Allied aircraft without having sustained appreciable damage. It was situated in a protected position which shielded it from most aerial bombardment. The captain in command of the Free French Commando unit to which I was attached, called his officers together to try and work out a solution. He pointed out the difficulties of a daylight attack in this sector and the serious losses the German gun batteries could inflict on our troops.[4]

Not surprisingly, the former saboteur in their midst had already reflected long and hard on these problems, and knowing the exact position of the source of the most dangerously effective fire, he proposed an unusual solution. Why not attempt a covert landing behind the German lines using a small commando force deployed on the banks of the river? Their boat could be laden with everything they would require to blow up the German blockhouse and De La Rochefoucauld willingly volunteered to take charge of the operation.

The officer in command was initially skeptical about the chances of the success of such a daring manoeuvre, but he was also aware of De La Rochefoucauld's past experience in the use of explosives when it came to the destruction of enemy targets. In the end—in the spirit of nothing ventured; nothing gained—he acquiesced and the necessary preparations were soon underway.

> Under cover of darkness, I set off in the Zodiac with three men, explosives, ignition wires, and submachine guns. It was a moonless night with a light rain falling: ideal conditions for our clandestine mission. There was no possible way we could use the motor, as it would have instantly signalled our presence so we moved in total silence using only our paddles. We had to make our way upriver for about three kilometres and knew we must also allow for another two hours at least to get to the exact position where we planned to come ashore..

> All went according to plan: after two hours we disembarked and immediately stashed the Zodiac. The blockhouse destined for destruction was about a kilometre away. We set off in single file; guided by my tiny pocket lamp and keeping a sharp lookout to avoid stepping on any landmines which the enemy had almost certainly laid around the perimeter of the blockhouse.

We finally spotted our target and at the same time, became aware of some unforeseen difficulties: the building was surrounded by a treeless area patrolled by a sentry. Then to further complicate the situation, around the perimeter of our target, we discerned a deep trench covered with camouflage netting. We would need to take out the sentry, of course, but this would have to be accomplished by stealth as opposed to gunfire which would have instantly given us away.

After carefully studying the lay of the land, I gave the men with me their instructions: two of them would position themselves on either side of the open enclosure; the third would remain with me and carry the explosives and ignition wires. My plan was to wait for the sentry to pass and—with any luck—quickly dispose of him in order to get close enough to be able to cut the netting with my knife. As a precautionary measure, the other two fellows would keep a close watch on my movements in the event that the sentry caught sight of me before I had a chance to take him out. Should this unwelcome eventuality come to pass, they would then immediately open fire to cover my withdrawal. This was, of course, the worst case scenario, as we would then have no alternative but to attempt to make an expeditious exit.[5]

But his proverbial luck had not yet deserted him. The darkness and constant downpour came as an additional bonus. To provide himself with greater protection from the elements, the sentry had sensibly pulled a hood up over his helmet and was keeping close to the wall which encircled the blockhouse. He was carrying his rifle, bandolier-style and looking down at his feet. This, of course, could only contribute to his vulnerability and ultimately to his undoing.

Each time the sentry disappeared around the side of the building, De La Rochefoucauld was able to make his way to the edge and cut away more of the netting until the opening was large enough to allow him to slip through and into the trench. So far... so good! Now it looked as if it would be safe to give the signal that once the sentry had turned the corner one last time, De La Rochefoucauld would be able to creep up on him from behind and their plan could proceed accordingly. His teammate with the equipment required for the detonation was to be ready to pass on the plastique with its attached ignition device which had been set for a delay of only seven minutes.

Once all was in readiness, as usual, things moved ahead at lightning speed. The sentry unwittingly made his final pass before I jumped him from behind, raked my knife across his throat and dragged his lifeless body close to the wall. Next came the explosives and ignition device. These I stuck firmly onto the blockhouse door before heading full tilt towards the perimeter wall. Grabbing on to the rope thrown over to me by my comrades, in near record time, I was hauled up and over to the other side.

We left the area at a dead run, no longer caring about potential landmines: we knew we only had a minute or two before the entire blockhouse would be blown sky high. Indeed, we had barely cleared five hundred yards before an enormous explosion echoed around us. Another mission accomplished!

Still running, we reached the spot on the riverbank where we had disembarked, and within seconds we were in the Zodiac and heading down the Gironde estuary towards our point of departure. Dawn was just breaking as we landed and were greeted by our euphoric captain who congratulated the team with an enthusiasm that fully compensated for his initial skepticism. He even went so far as to announce that he had every intention of proposing all of us for the Croix de Guerre. For our part, we were simply happy to have come through our 'adventure' without a scratch. In fact, at that particular moment, our only ambition was to find a bed and catch up on some well-earned sleep.

From our perspective, Operation Blockhouse had appeared to be a great success; but to be absolutely certain how much damage we had actually inflicted, we had to bide our time until the general offensive was launched against Graves Point. Then, and only then, would we know whether or not we had caused enough havoc to prevent the surviving occupants of the blockhouse from mounting any appreciable opposition to our advancing troops.[6]

As it turned out, the answer was not long in coming. At dawn on April 15, 1945, the zone held by the Germans became the target of heavy Allied bombardment.[7] A few tanks advanced with the objective of opening up a path through the minefields of "No Man's Land". Then, in the late afternoon, De La Rochefoucauld's unit began its own advance, and they soon discovered—to their enormous satisfaction—that not a single shot had been fired from the fortification they had successfully managed to obliterate. In the captain's words, it was a case of "Bravo Operation Blockhouse!"

By the same evening, French troops had broken through the German lines and within two days had advanced to the Verdon River. This was followed by another two days of sustained combat. The Germans were resisting with extraordinary determination. These seasoned troops, unaffiliated in any way with any SS units, were among the last of the German Wehrmacht whose loyalty to the

Fatherland repudiated any thoughts of surrender until all other options had run their course.

By the same token, in spite of their comparatively meagre firepower, the French troops forged ahead with bravery and determination and slowly but surely were gaining ground. The following day, the enemy was forced to fall back on its remaining positions on the River Verdon and within twenty-four hours, the last enemy forces at Graves Point had finally surrendered.

But for De La Rochefoucauld, these days of armed conflict were precipitously cut short. The luck that had attached itself to him limpet-like through so many narrow escapes had suddenly deserted him. On April 19th, he suffered a severe knee injury when he was struck by shrapnel from a landmine. He was carried off on a stretcher, first to a field hospital and later evacuated to Bordeaux for surgery, which resulted in the successful replacement of his kneecap with an implant fashioned out of silver alloy.

For his convalescence, he was dispatched to Rochefort-sur-Mer north of Royan and it was here that he learned of the tragic and untimely loss of his beloved older brother, Henri ; killed in action in Alsace while advancing towards the German border with the Second Division of the French Forces.

The depth of my sorrow was only compounded by the frustration of sitting helplessly on the sidelines instead of being part of the fighting along the Rhine. As I had not seen my family since my Paris interlude in the early winter of 1944, it seemed perfectly reasonable to request a temporary absence from my military duties. I was soon pronounced "cured" and was granted a month's leave.

It came as an enormous source of joy to me to find my entire family gathered together with my parents. Given the circumstances, it was a deeply emotional reunion for everyone: my mother and father had both been devastated by Henri's death. Together, we shared this great sadness, and at the same time, we marvelled at seeing one another, nine brothers and sisters reunited. As for myself, I could scarcely overcome my surprise at finding myself still alive and able to rejoice in the news of Germany's surrender.[8]

This 1945 safe conduct leaflet for the use of German soldiers who wished to surrender signed by Dwight D. Eisenhower was widely circulated.

15 AFTERMATH

The four weeks of De La Rochefoucauld's well-earned convalescent leave in the bosom of his family passed all too quickly and were followed in short order by a completely new prospect. From a life of survival in enemy-occupied territory; he suddenly found himself precipitously transferred to the ranks of the victorious Allied Occupying Force quartered in Germany. After briefly rejoining his regiment of dragoons, he was soon re-assigned to serve as aide-de-camp to General Noiret, the Assistant Commander-in-Chief of the French Forces in Germany, whose headquarters had been set up in Germany's oldest city, Trier, situated on the banks of the Moselle River.[1]

In his capacity as Noiret's ADC, De La Rochefoucauld accompanied the general in the course of his extensive post-war travels throughout Germany and makes particular reference to one memorable trip to the ruins of the city of Berlin.

> We had occasion to meet many Soviet officers—even Marshals—including the legendary Zhukov,[2] the celebrated hero of Stalingrad, who was equally renowned for his immoderate enthusiasm for vodka. In conjunction with one of our visits, it occurred to Marshal Zhukov that he and his staff should hold a small reception to celebrate Franco-Russian

friendship. It was, of course, incumbent upon me to accompany General Noiret, the guest of honour, and I admit to the fact that I felt no reluctance whatever about the prospect of fulfilling my duties in this regard. In fact, I anticipated it with the greatest of pleasure.

On arrival, we discovered that the gathering included perhaps thirty guests—all of them Russian officers with the exception of General Noiret, an interpreter, and myself. The interpreter dutifully introduced us to our host, and upon hearing the name De La Rochefoucauld, the Marshal let out a roar of raucous laughter. Perhaps the interpreter had pronounced it too quickly? In any event, it turned out that Zhukov had mistaken my name for La Roche-Zhukov. Here stood a distant relative in his presence and this became the cause for even greater celebration. I was instantly proclaimed a member of the Zhukov clan and embraced in true Russian style, which, incidentally, included a hearty smack on the lips. For the duration of the evening, I became known to all the Russian officers present as La Roche-Zhukov.

A formal dinner awaited us and we were ushered to the table. Each of us had a goblet placed in front of him, with waiters standing respectfully behind. The Marshal had barely begun his speech of welcome in our honour, which our interpreter had duly translated for us, when Zhukov decided that we should all stand up and drink a toast to the health of the Allies—one and all. At the name of each country, our goblets were re-filled, and it was, of course, de rigeur to drain it—Russian style—to the last drop in a single gulp.

It requires precious little imagination to picture the condition of those assembled by the time a toast to the valour of the tenth Allied nation was proposed. Prudently, I had followed the shining example of General Noiret, who emptied half the contents of his goblet onto the oriental carpet before each toast. For their part, our Soviets hosts were averse to practising any such restraint and the results were self-evident.

As the evening drew inevitably to a close, the Marshal—more than a little unsteady on his feet—bade us farewell and accompanied us to the front steps, which he descended with some difficulty, despite the support of two of his aides. The chauffeur proceeded to ceremoniously open the rear door of the staff limousine and the Marshal clambered in, only to end up sprawled face down on the pavement on the other side of the car. Following a frantic rush to rescue the Savior of Stalingrad, the Marshall was at last installed more or less upright on the back seat and the car drove off.

As good form dictates, it goes without saying that neither General Noiret nor I displayed any outward signs of having observed unbecoming behaviour on the part of the Marshal. It was incumbent upon us to exercise our powers of self-control to the fullest extent—at least until safely installed in the privacy of our own vehicle.[3]

It had indeed been a night to remember—one of countless memories belonging to what Canadian war artist, Charles Comfort once aptly referred to as 'a time out of time'. The world had been forever changed and turning back the clock was not an option.

EPILOGUE

In concluding his memoir, Robert De La Rochefoucauld makes reference to the post-war malaise that so many of those who had seen action experienced after the fact. For the most part, it was a difficult period of adjustment for all concerned. For some, the process was relatively brief; while for others, it was a protracted exercise in complexity.

Having served for almost a year in war-torn Germany in his capacity as aide-de-camp, in May 1946, holding the rank of captain, De La Rochefoucauld left General Noiret and returned to France to attend to the required formalities that accompanied the process of demobilization. To his great astonishment, he discovered that thanks to some sort of bizarre administrative foul-up, his name had been listed as a Reservist with the Naval Commandos. Robert De La Rochefoucauld, whose one and only experience at sea had been the memorable evacuation from France to England by submarine two years earlier. It was difficult to imagine a more ludicrous designation. In any event, following his demobilization, he was immediately sent off to participate in a course at the Centre for Special Services situated at Cercotte, a small village near Orléans. Here, he had occasion to come upon some old covert operations friends who had—like himself—been fortunate enough to have survived the war more or less intact.

Together they decided to join forces and become members of the Franco-Anglo-Belgian Fraternity of Parachutist Agents, where De La Rochefoucauld's unexpected appearance once again created something of a stir among a few of his former comrades-at-arms in England who had long since mourned his passing. Silver knee-cap notwithstanding, to everyone's mutual delight, there he stood—very much alive and well and toasts must be drunk accordingly.[1]

At some point during his stint at Cercotte, De La Rochefoucauld was asked if he would volunteer to spend three months in Indochina training a battalion of shock troops in commando tactics. At that juncture, France's regular Army was not yet well-versed in this type of warfare. It should come as no surprise, then, that this idea was instantly appealing to De La Rochefoucauld—and the fact that, by coincidence, the regional Commander-in-Chief in Indochina was none other than his uncle, General Leclerc de Hautecloque.[2] Ironically, the two never had occasion to meet during the course of this five-month assignment in Indochina, although De La Rochefoucauld mentions having taken part in a few commando operations against the Viet Minh.

The main strategy in the parts of Indochina still held by the French was to create strongholds, from which they could attempt to control the neighbouring sectors. The Viet strategy was to attack these posts as well as targeting convoys of arms and food. It fell to De La Rochefoucauld to train a subversive commando unit which, disguised as Viet Minhs, would set up traps similar to those of their adversaries. The objective was to engage and ruthlessly destroy all enemy groups they encountered. This was by no means an assignment for the faint of heart.

Nor did reports of these sorties pass unnoticed upstairs. Before long, certain senior authorities demanded explanations. Although the principle behind these operations was to inflict significant losses on the insurgents, there were certain high-ranking officials who were adamantly opposed to the guerrilla tactics being employed. "The results are plain to see," De La Rochefoucauld was told, "but this type of operation simply does not conform to the tradition of the French Army." Given his rank, the response he gave was nothing short of audacious, however he felt honour-bound to present his considered opinion that in the final analysis the French Army and those commanding it, would soon have to decide whether they wanted to win the war or face defeat.

It goes without saying that neither his views on the matter, nor his lack of hesitation in expressing them were well received and within a month he was on his way back to France. It was only sometime later that he discovered—to his surprise—that those in control of operations on the ground in Indochina had continued the use of the commando tactics and that, in the end, guerrilla warfare was not necessarily deemed contrary to the tradition of the French Army. In hindsight, it appears to have been a case of expedience in the face of desperation, for the nine-year French presence in Indochina eventually ended in a humiliating defeat and withdrawal in 1953.[3]

Once back in France, De La Rochefoucauld decided that perhaps the time had finally come to attempt to put his past behind him and settle into a career in business, or at least try his hand at it. Not surprisingly, his good intentions were to no avail. The daily round and common task of office life in Paris soon palled; and the lure of combining business and travel took him first to the Cameroon for three years, followed by two more years in Venezuela. The proverbial rolling stone.

The erstwhile man-of-action found himself drawn once more to the Special Services Centre at Cercotte, where in 1956 he was asked to participate as a volunteer on an assignment that particularly appealed to his unfettered sense of adventure. His role would involve being parachuted into the Sinaï as leader of a team designated to rescue downed aviators. But, to his chagrin, just as he and his men were preparing for their imminent departure, word came through that unforeseen political developments had created a precipitous change in plan. There would be no further need of the team's assistance, nor of its fearless leader's services.

His days of living on the edge had ground inexorably to a halt and he was left with the only choice open to a man of his character: to come to terms with the future and make the most of it.

Photo taken during De La Rochefoucauld's post-war interlude under the African sun in Cameroon, French West African. Courtesy the De La Rochefoucauld family archives.

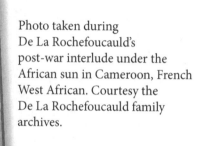

Robert De La Rochefoucauld pays a post-war visit to the hotel in Auxerres whose owner—a member of the Resistance—had helped Robert to make one of his many narrow escapes. Courtesy the De La Rochefoucauld family archives.

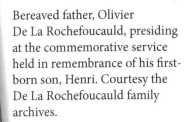

Photo of Captain
De La Rochefoucauld taken
at Villeneuve while on
convalescent leave from the
Army, May 1945. Courtesy
the De La Rochefoucauld
family archives.

Bereaved father, Olivier
De La Rochefoucauld, presiding
at the commemorative service
held in remembrance of his first-
born son, Henri. Courtesy the
De La Rochefoucauld family
archives.

Family service of remembrance for eldest son,
Henri De La Rochefoucauld tragically killed in action in Alsace,
1945. General Philippe Leclerc in uniform pays his respects.
Courtesy the De La Rochefoucauld family archives.

More than a quarter century after his wartime exploits, Count
Robert De La Rochefoucauld is awarded the medal of the Legion
of Honour by French president, Valéry Giscard d'Estaing in 1974.
Courtesy the De La Rochefoucauld family archives.

POSTSCRIPT

Count Robert De La Rochefoucauld's 2002 memoir—*La Liberté, C'est mon plaisir*—bears witness to the makings of a courageous young patriot whose indomitable spirit and personal panache carried him forward into a long and honourable future. At the age of 78, it was with justifiable pride that he was able to list in his memoir the following decorations received as a result of his steadfast dedication to his country and his unswerving belief in the cause of freedom:

The Medal of the Resistance
The Military Cross
The Order of Merit
The Legion of Honour
The Distinguished Conduct Medal

Robert De La Rochefoucauld dedicated his 2002 memoir to his wife, Bernadette and to his four children, Astrid, Constance, Hortense and Jean who had all encouraged him to set down his wartime memories for them as well as for the next generation—his grandchildren Maxime, Timothé, Caroline, Benjamin, Amélie, Armand, Eléanore, Diane, Margaux and Audrey. It is a treasured legacy.

He concludes his memoir by paying homage to the numerous members of his family circle who were ready and willing to join the fight for freedom—'pour la liberté'. First and foremost he commends his beloved mother, who had listened to De Gaulle's call to arms on 18 June 1940 and infused the spirit of resistance among all the members of her family for the duration of the Occupation. He also pays tribute to his older brother, Henri, who fought bravely with France's Second Battalion during the advance towards Germany and died for his country in Alsace in 1944, His brother-in-law, Albert de Schonen who served with the Jedburghs as a combatant is also included, as is his distinguished uncle, Philippe de Hauteclocque, better known as Marshal Philippe Leclerc. His personal accolades also extend to several others in the family circle who counted themselves among those present and accounted for in the struggle for the liberation of France. *La liberté, C'est mon plaisir* writ large!

Robert photographed with his bride on their wedding day. Courtesy the De La Rochefoucauld family archives.

Photo of the author of 2002 wartime memoir,
La Liberté, c'est mon plaisir. Courtesy the
De La Rochefoucauld family archives.

APPENDIX I

An abridged and translated chronology of events in the Second World War history of the French Resistance. (Adapted from Chronologie, pp. 539-546. *Histoire de la Résistance 1940-1945 :To obey is a betrayal. To disobey is to serve* by Olivier Wieviorka, Éditions Perrin, Paris 2013.)

1940

17 June	Édmond Michelet in Brive, Charles Tillon in Bordeaux distribute their first political pamphlets aimed at encouraging the Résistance movement.
18 June	Charles de Gaulle makes his now famous London broadcast; representatives of the French Communist Party begin negotiating for the renewed publication of "L'Humanité"—the French Communist Party newspaper.
20 June	Étienne Achavanne commits the Occupation's first act of sabotage by cutting telephone lines.
22 June	French-German Armistice is signed.
July	Winston Churchill creates the Special Operations Executive (SOE), the goal of which is to actively undertake acts of sabotage throughout occupied Europe.
1 July	André Dewavrin, known as "(Major) Passy", is appointed Chief of the 'Deuxième et Troisième Bureaux'. The 2e Bureau—in existence as early as 1936—was an organization ostensibly designed to combat Communist and Resistance activities aimed at

the Nazi Occupation. On the surface, it successfully presented the appearance of sustaining its legitimate role, while simultaneously working covertly with MI6, MI9, and the SOE.

10 July	The French Parliament accords full powers to Marshal Philippe Pétain.
14 July	The BBC broadcasts the first of a series of radio programs aimed at listeners in France
18 July	Debut of the BBC radio emissions by the Free French.
7 August	Churchill-de Gaulle Accords/Agreements; Great Britain officially recognizes the Free French Forces.
3 October	First Law relating to Jews enacted.
27 October	De Gaulle in Brazzaville forms the "Defense of the Empire Council".
November	Henri Frenay's "Manifesto" announcing the founding of "Movement for National Liberation"; founding of "Freedom-France",--later re-named "The Sniper"—publication by the Free University of "Little Wings" in northern France around Pas de Calais.
9 November	Disbanding of all Management and Union organizations.
11 November	Demonstration by Paris secondary and university students at les Étoiles and on the Champs Élysées.
15 November	Union Movement's 'Manifesto'.
25 November	First issue of "La Liberté".
December	Creation of 'The Civilian and Military Organization'. An appeal to all French people to desert the streets.

1941

January	Creation of a Socialist Action Committee for the Occupied Zone.
21 January	Resistance hero, Honoré d'Estienne d'Orves is betrayed and arrested.
30 March	Formation of the 'Socialist Action Committee" for the Southern Zone.

23 April	Law enacted to nationalize the police forces.
5 May	First parachute drop into France of an agent assigned to F Section of the SOE—WT Georges Bégué or George Noble.
15 May	The French Communist Party sends out a backdated appeal for the creation of a National Front for French Independence.
27 May	Beginning of the miners' strike in the north (Pas-de-Calais region).
June	First issue of *Bulletin of the Volunteers for Freedom*.
2 June	Second Law relating to Jews enacted.
10 June	End of the Miners' Strike in the North—total work force back at work.
22 June	Beginning of 'Operation Barbarossa'—Germany's invasion of Soviet Russia.
July	First issue of *Libération-sud*.
14 July	First issue of *Defence of France*.
27 August	Paris 'Special Section' retroactively condemns three Communists to death.
24 September	De Gaulle forms the National French Committee.
20 October	Jean Moulin arrives in London.
21 October	Execution of 48 hostages following assassinations in Nantes and Bordeaux.
23 October	De Gaulle condemns the strategy of individual assassinations in a radio broadcast.
25 October	First meeting between de Gaulle and Jean Moulin in London.
November	Merger of two movements: *Liberté and National Libération* which is named "Combat" after the newspaper of that name.
6 November	Parachute drop by Agent Leon Morandat. (Code names: Yvon, Leo, Amalphe)
December	First issues of *The Sniper and Combat*.
7 December	The United States enters the War following the Japanese attack on Pearl Harbour.

1942

2 January   Jean Moulin parachuted into South of France.

20 February   *Les Éditions de Minuit* publishes *Le Silence de la Mer* by Vercors.

27-28 February   Destruction of radar station at Bruneval.

27 March   Departure of the first convoy of French Jewish deportees des-
                     tined for Auschwitz.

17 April   General Henri Giraud escapes from German prison near
                     Dresden.

28 April   Christian Pineau returns from London with General de Gaulle's
                     Manifesto.

1 May   Demonstrations in the Southern Zone.

14 July   Popular demonstrations in the Southern Zone.

14 July   'Free France' is re-christened as 'Fighting France'.

1 August   Demonstration by housewives in the rue Daguerre in Paris.

23 August   Pastoral letter delivered from respected cleric, Monseigneur
                     Saliège protesting the Jewish roundups and detention.

4 September   Enactment of first Vichy Government law on compulsory la-
                     bour. October Accord reached in London between the Free
                     French and the various Resistance organizations in south-
                     ern France for the purpose of coordination with those in the
                     Occupied Zone.

13 October   Strikes against the deportation order enacted by the Vichy gov-
                     ernment as part of its Compulsory Work Program.

November   Formation of a co-ordination Committee involving Resistance
                     movements in the southern zone.

November   Creation of a Free French Air Force and Naval Operations
                     Service (SOAM).

8 November   British and American landing in North Africa.

11 November   Operation Case *Anton*—the German take-over of the French
                     Southern Zone known as Vichy France.

27 November	French Navy scuttles its fleet in Toulon Harbour
24 December	Assassination of French Admiral François Darlan.
26 December	General Henri Giraud named Civil and Military Commander of Free French troops in North Africa.

1943

6 January	Civilian mob overcomes German guards supervising boarding at Montluçon station of large group of men destined for Germany under the obligatory work service program. All detainees escape.
11 January	Fernand Grenier, representative of the French Communist Party, arrives for meetings in London.
26 January	Amalgamation of the three largest Resistance movements in southern France.
30 January	Founding of the Milice—a collaborationist police force aligned with the Nazis in the south of France.
2 February	German surrender at Stalingrad.
16 February	Vichy defines three age categories for the Obligatory Work Service.
21 February	De Gaulle orders the creation of a National Resistance Council.
26 March	Co-ordination committee established for the Northern zone.
April	Creation of the Office of Aerial Operations
27 May	First Meeting of the National Resistance Council in Paris.
30 May	Arrival of General de Gaulle in Algeria.
21 June	Arrest of Jean Moulin and other highly placed Resistance figures.
25 June	Creation of a Central Committee of Resistance movements.
9 September	Uprising of Corsican partisans.
4 October	Liberation of Corsica.
11 November	Nation-wide demonstrations throughout France.
13 November	Destruction of the artillery range at Grenoble.

1944

January	Several Resistance organizations amalgamate.
15 January	*Defense of France*, periodical- publication, prints 450,000 copies of its issue #43.
20 January	Vichy regime creates special military courts to try captured resistants.
February	Increase in guerilla activity on the Haute Savoie's Glières plateau.
15 March	National Council of Resistance program is adopted.
26 March	German forces comb the Glières plateau in hopes of rooting out all Resistance forces.
2 April	Massacre at Ascq where 86 Frenchmen were executed by Waffen-SS *Hitlerjugend* troops in retaliation for railway sabotage.
21 April	Central Committee of Resistance defines public administration, responsibilities during and after the Liberation.
30 May	General Marie-Pierre Koenig is recognized by the Allies as the Commander-in-Chief of the FFI or French Forces of the Interior.
6 June	Allied Landing in Normandy. Resistance follows established-plan of action.
6 June	De Gaulle's BBC broadcast to the people of France followed by the unofficial anthem of the French Resistance—*Le Chant des Partisans*.
8-9 June	Entrapment of guerilla forces in the Vercors Mountains in the vicinity of Grenoble.
9 June	Mass execution by hangings of 120 civilian men and boys at Tulle conducted by a unit of the *Waffen SS*.
10 June	General Koenig orders an abatement in guerilla activities; Germans attack guerilla forces at Mont-Mouchet; German Division known as *'Das Reich'* engages in a massacre at Oradour-sur-Glane.
14 June	De Gaulle visits troops in Normandy.

18 June	German attack on the Resistance forces at St-Marcel. Guerillas disperse.
25 July	Beginning of 'Operation Cobra' resulting in a break-through towards Avranche.
4 August	Liberation of Rennes.
10 August	Beginning of the Railway Workers' Strike in Paris.
15 August	Landing of combined French and American troops in Provence.
15 August	Beginning of the Parisian Police Strike.
16 August	Hitler orders the German retreat.
17 August	Departure of the last convoy train of Jews destined for extermination.
18 Augus	Unions in Paris issue directive for a General Strike.
19 August	Beginning of the Parisian uprising.
20 August	Liberation of Toulouse.
21 August	Insurrection in Marseille, Limoges liberated.
22 August	Liberation of Grenoble.
25 August	German surrender in Paris.
26 August	Liberation Parade in Paris.
3 September	Liberation of Lyon; Liberation of Lille.
9 September	Formation of new government under Charles de Gaulle.
30 September	New ordinance governing the Press.
28 October	Dissolution of the Milice.
23 November	Liberation of Strasbourg.
16 December	Germans launch a major offensive in the Ardennes.

1945

16 January	Nationalization of the Renault automobile factories.

9 April	Nationalization of Air France.
29 April	First round of municipal elections.
8 May	Surrender of Germany.
13 May	Second round of municipal elections in France.
4 -19 October	Laws enacted governing social security.
21 October	Referendum and elections for the National Assembly.
21 November	Formation of Charles de Gaulle's new government.
2 December	Nationalization of Credit Unions and the Bank of France.

APPENDIX II

Secret Second World War stations – Special Operations Executive

*A partial but incomplete list of Special Operations Executive sites located in the UK from 1940-1945.

SOE/PWE Toddington Rectory

In July 1940, two French stations were established here; F1, Radio Inconnu and F2, Radio Travail. Both were of a subversive nature.

These top-secret Freedom Stations were referred to as 'Research Units' and even Tradesmen doing maintenance on the premises were kept under escort at all times.

SOE/SIS St. Ermin Hotel

St. Ermin Hotel headquarters of the SIS's Section D (March 1938) which amalgamated with the War Office Research Group and Military Intelligence to establish the SOE's first base of operation using the name 'Statistical Research Department' and operating under the direction of Sir Hugh Dalton as of 22 July 1940.

SOE Baker Street

Michael House on Baker Street was the head office of Marks & Spencer. The SOE were given the use of limited office space by the company for the duration. The SOE took up occupation on 31 October 1940.

SOE 64 Baker Street/Broadstone Place.

The SOE entrance to 64 Baker Street was in Broadstone Place.

SOE Norgeby House, 83 Baker Street (also Marks & Spencer

property) Norgeby House, Baker Street was the home of the Signals Directorate (Secret Intelligence Service), responsible for the SIS communications networks and served as the SOE radio service prior to the establishment of the SOE's own communications network beginning in June 1942. No. 83 also housed the offices of Section F where it's Director, Colonel Maurice Buckmaster was assisted by Vera Atkins in orchestrating activities in the French sector.

SOE F Section, Montague Mansions

The premises of Montague Mansions were used for interview and briefing by SOE F Section.

SOE F section, Orchard Court

Orchard Court housed interview and briefing rooms for SOE F Section (1943).

SOE Bikenhall Mansions

Dutch Section briefing rooms (1943) used by agents: Golf, Hockey & Tennis.

SOE Chiltern Court

Chiltern court was the 'Holding House' for the Norwegian Section in London. During 1942 the flat was used by Poulson, Helberg, Kjelstrup and Haugland before they were dispatched to Norway.

SOE STS2 Bellasis House
Italian Section Country House (1941)

SOE STS1 Brockhall Hall
Spanish Section Country House (1941)

SOE STS3 Stodham Park
Danish and Norwegian Section—Country House

SOE STS 6 West Court
West Court, Finchampstead
Czech/Dutch Country House (1941)

SOE Addington House

SOE Gaynes Hall
Gaynes Hall was requisitioned from the Duberley family and used by the Special Operations Executive (SOE). It was given the code name 'Station 61' and served as the Headquarters of the Air Liaison Officers as well as temporary quarters for agents waiting for clearance before being dropped into Occupied Europe. In 1942, as a Parachute Container Packing Centre, the station was staffed by close to 350 workers and by 1945 had produced a total of 78,500 containers.

SOE STS52 Grendon Hall

SOE Station 53a was responsible for the liaison and organisation of resistance Groups in France. From August 1942, Grendon Underwood wireless station run by MI 6 handled SOE radio traffic.

SOE STS 53b Poundon House

SOE Hazells Hall

SOE stores were also situated at Hazells Hall. Arms, ammunition radio sets and other supplies were delivered to Resistance groups from the Arctic Circle to the Mediterranean.

SOE Woodbury Hall

Requisitioned for use as a hostel for the R. A. F. pilots using the Tempsford Aerodrome.

SOE Tetworth Hall

Requisitioned for use as a hostel for the R. A. F. pilots using the Tempsford Aerodrome.

SOE Harrington Airfield

801st Bomber Group

SOE Desborough

84 OTU RAF Desborough

SOE Cheddington

801st Bomber Group

RAF Tempsford

Tempsford which was a dedicated SOE airfield for the sole use of Special Operations Squadrons, No 138 and 161 which flew a variety of multi-engine aircraft such as the Halifax, Whitley, and Hudson. Auxiliary hangers were erected for the use of single-engine Lysanders.

SOE Gibraltar Farm

Number 138 and 161 Squadrons operated from the base using a variety of aircraft. Designated to drop or pick up agents, collect VIPs and deliver supplies.

RAF Tangmere*

Both No. 138 and 161 Squadrons were equipped with the Lysander Mark III which operated as far south as Perigueux and as far east as the Jura. All outbound and inbound operations for France were located at Tangmere.

SOE Tangmere Cottage

SOE Heigham Holmes

The marshes at Heigham Holmes were used as a secret airfield between 1940 to 1944 by Special Operations Executive Lysanders ferrying agents to occupied Europe.

SOE Y Station Chicksands Priory near Shefford, was acquired by the Crown in 1936 and was operational as a listening station for the duration of the war.

SOE MD1 Workshop Bedford

MD1 Cecil Vandepeer Clarke's workshop at the rear of 172-3 Tavistock Street. Codenamed 'Area K', it housed the Special Operations Demolition School.

SOE Home of John Gibbs

The Rectory, Tingrith, Home of John Gibbs (Luton News and Leagrave Press.)

SOE Luton News printers

The *Nachrichten* propaganda operations designed for German readership (*Nachrichten* meaning News) began approximately a month before D-Day with nightly print runs of 100,000 copies. By D-Day 1 million copies of *Nachrichten* a day were being produced and packed into 100-leaflet bundles.

SOE Leagrave Press

Production and packing facility for the SOE print works. This factory was sold to The Murdoch Group in 1988 and demolished shortly thereafter.

SOE MD 1 test site

The now demolished Bedford School swimming pool was used to test the MD1 'limpet mine' designed by 'Nobby' Clarke in the secret SOE workshop in Tavistock Street.

SOE MD 1 Limpet mine factory Bedford

During the winter of 1939 Nobby manufactured the first 250 limpets in his Tavistock Street workshop. The second order was for 1,000 so additional space was needed.

SOE MD 1 Limpet Mine test site

The field trials took place in Bedford Baths, the property of Bedford Modern School.

SOE Station 9, The Frythe

The SOE took over the Frythe in July 1940, naming it Station IX. Research was conducted into explosives, sabotage, camouflage, weapons and possibly chemical weapons.

SOE MD 1 The Firs, Whitchurch

The Firs, Whitchurch, near Aylesbury, Buckinghamshire where Nobby Clarke worked from Spring 1942 on various weaponry projects with Stuart Macrae. The Firs was the home of the Great Eastern project.

SOE School of Cryptography

SOE School of Cryptography, St Andrews Road lodgings, probable location for reception for trainees into the Cryptography School (Jan 1942) under the Command of Major Masters.

SOE STS31a The House in the Woods
The House in the Woods was one of 11 houses within the Montague family's Beaulieu Estate used by SOE It served as the Officers' Mess.

SOE STS 32 Briggens Park
Polish 'Finishing School' 1941.

SOE STS Rhinefield House
Rhinefield House was one of 11 houses within the Beaulieu Estate used by SOE

SOE STS 32 Hertford House
(aka 'The Fisheries') Requisitioned in 1941.

SOE STS 32a Saltmarsh
Administration house Saltmarsh was another of the 11 houses within the grounds of the Beaulieu Estate used by the SOE

SOE STS 32b Blackbridge House
Blackbridge Administration House was also located within the Beaulieu Estate.

SOE STS33 The House On The Shore
Beaulieu Estate property

SOE STS 35 Vineyards
Vineyards House was within the Beaulieu Estate complex comprised of 11 buildings given over to the use of the SOE

SOE Brockenhurst Goods Yard

SOE STS36 Boarmans
Boarmans was used as a 'finishing school' for women agents.

SOE STS37a Warren House
Warren, now Blackwater House, taught microphotography and also served as a General 'finishing school'. Used as an administrative house 1941.

SOE Fawley Court
Fawley Court home of the SOE Signals Training Unit for training high speed, accurate Morse Code transmission, using only highly qualified ciphers.

SOE RF Section 1 Dorset Square
Section house for the Charles de Gaulle known as RF (French) Section HQ. and home of the National Council of the Resistance chief, Pierre Brossolette.

SOE Milton Hall

SOE Jedburgh Training School
Training both British and American agents in guerilla warfare techniques.

SOE/SIS & ISRB Inverlair Lodge
The ISRB 'Workshops' was established to create a 'holding tank' for failed agents who could not be posted elsewhere until sensitive operations they had been trained for had been completed.

SOE STS4 (& STS7) Winterfold

Winterfold became the home of the SOE Students Assessment Board (SAB) in June 1943 after the high rate of rejected students became a burden to the training programme.

SOE STS 5 Wanborough manor

Wanborough Manor, near Guildford was the starting point for many agents traveling north to STS 21 Scottish training school. French Section Country House (1941) Agent: Lt.Marcus Bloom.

SOE Station 6 Bride Hall

Weapons acquisition section. In July 1946 this station was absorbed by Station 12 Aston House.

SOE STS 6 West Court

West Court, Finchampstead Czech/Dutch Section Country House (1941)

SOE Station7a Bondex Cleaning Factory

SOE/SCU Wireless Section

Production facility based in the Bondex Knitting Factory. This facility was later used in conjunction with the Bondex Cleaning Works and the Ruislip Cigarette Factory.

SOE/SCU Ruislip cigarette works

SOE/SCU Wireless Section Production facility based in the Ruislip cigarette factory, used in conjunction with the Bondex Cleaning Works and the Bondex Knitting factory at Wembley.

SOE Station7a Bondex Knitting Factory
Radio assembly section. Post-July 1946 this station was absorbed by Station 12 Aston House.

SOE Station 7b Yeast-Vite factory
Inter-Services Research Bureau (Station VIIb)—Post July 1946 this station was absorbed by Station 12 Aston House.

SOE Station 7c Allensor's joinery factory
Allensor's joinery factory, King George's Avenue. Wireless Section Research. Post July 1946 this station was absorbed by Station 12 Aston House.

SOE Station IXa Queen Mary reservoir, Staines
Station IX A was used for the testing of prototype water-borne equipment. This ranged from one man float packs to the Welfreighter midget submarine.

SOE Station 9c, Fishguard Bay Hotel
Fishguard Bay Hotel was used as a field testing centre for water craft.

SOE Station 11, Gorhambury house thought to be used as accommodation.

SOE Station 12, Aston House

SOE Aston House Station XI
The house became the officers ' mess of a unit of SOE. engaged in the design, production and testing of weapons and explosives for use in guerrilla warfare and sabotage operations.

SOE Station 14, Briggens Park.
SOE forged documentation section and sabotage training school.

SOE Station 15a, 56 Queen's Gate
Linked C, Camouflage Section—prototypes

PWE The Rookery
PWE The Rookery—Each of the broadcasting and propaganda teams were known as Research Units or RUs.

PWE The Mount
PWE The Mount propaganda team.

* The PWE/ POLITICAL WARFARE EXECUTIVE included staff from the Ministry of Information, the propaganda elements of the Special Operations Executive, and the BBC. Its main headquarters was at Woburn Abbey with London offices at the BBC's Bush House. As the Political Warfare Executive was a secret department, it was publicly referred to as the Political Intelligence Department (PID).

The main forms of propaganda used were disseminated through radio broadcasts and the wholesale production of leaflets. The PWE also created a number of clandestine radio stations to deliver its subversive messages aimed at German listeners. As well, it broadcast reliable news and information on events in Germany and the occupied countries, including intelligence gleaned from other services and agencies, POW interrogations, and newspapers obtained from occupied countries, and bombing raid photo analysis. This latter source was used to broadcast lists of streets (and even individual houses) that had been destroyed and on occasion to mock up faked "real time" reports of actual raids.

After D-Day most of PWE's propaganda staff transferred to the Psychological Warfare Division (PWD/SHAEF) of SHAEF.

SOURCES AND BIBLIOGRAPHY

Archival Sources

Churchill Archives Centre, Churchill College, Cambridge, UK.

Imperial War Museum, London.

Memorial Leclerc/ Musée Jean Moulin, Paris.

Musée de La Resistance Nationale, Paris.

National Archives, Kew, UK.

Related Bibliographic Sources

Amoureoux, Henri. *La Vie des Français sous l'Occupation*. Paris, 1990.

Andrew, Christopher. *Her Majesty's Secret Service—The Making of the British Intelligence Community*. New York: Viking Press, 1986.

Argyle, Ray. *The Paris Game: Charles de Gaulle, the Liberation of Paris, and the Gamble that Won France*. Toronto: Dundurn Press, 2014.

Aubrac, L. *Outwitting the Gestapo*. Lincoln: University of Nebraska Press, 1993.

Azéma, Jean-Pierre. *De Munich à la Libération—1938-1944.* Paris: Editions du Seuil, 1979.

Aziz, Philippe, *Histoire de la Gestapo en France—Livre noir de la traison.* Paris, 1984.

Bailey, Roderick, *Forgotten Voices of the Secret War: An Inside History of Special Operations During the Second World War.* London, Ebury Press, 2008.

Beavan, Colin, *"Operation Jedburgh" : D-Day and America's First Shadow War.* Google Books, 2006.

Berthon, Simon & Potts, Joanna. *Warlords: An Extraordinary Re-Creation of World War II Through the Eyes and Minds of Hitler, Churchill, Roosevelt and Stalin.* London, Thistle Publishing 2013.

Binney, M. *Secret War Heroes: Men of the Special Operations Executive.* London, 2005.

Boyce, Frederic & Everett, Douglas. SOE: *The Scientific Secrets.* Stroud, UK: The History Press, 2011.

Brown, Anthony Cave. *"C" The Secret Life of Sir Stewart Menzies, Spymaster to Winston Churchill.* New York: Macmillan, 1987.

Buckmaster, Maurice J. *Specially Employed: The Story of British Aid to French Patriots of the Resistance.* London: Batchworth, 1952.

Buckmaster, Maurice. *They Fought Alone: The Story of British Agents in France.* London: W. W. Norton, 1958.

Butler, Josephine. *Churchill's Secret Agent. Josephine Butler. Codename " Jay Bee":* Toronto: Ashburton, 1983.

Beevor, Anthony & Cooper, Artemis. *Paris: After the Liberation 1944-1949.* London: Hamish Hamilton, 1994.

Betz, Albrecht, Martens, Stephan. *Les Intellectuels et L'Occupation.* Paris: Hamish Hamilton, 2004.

Boxshall, Lieutenant Colonel E. G. *Chronology of SOE Operations with the Resistance in France during World War II. 1960.* A typescript copy at Pearl Witherington-Cornioley library, also available at the Valençay library.

Clutton-Brock, Oliver. *RAF Evaders: The Complete Story of RAF Escapees and Their Escape Lines, Western Europe, 1940-1945.* London: Grub Street Publishing, 2012.

Cobb, Matthew. *Eleven Days in August: The Liberation of Paris in 1944.* New York: Simon & Schuster, 2013.

Cobb, Richard. *French and Germans, Germans and French.* London: Brandeis, 1983.

Cookridge, E. *Inside SOE The Story of Special Operations in Western Europe, 1940-1945.* London: Arthur Baker Ltd., 1966.

Cunningham, Cyril. *Beaulieu: The Finishing School for Secret Agents.* London: Pen & Sword, 1998.

Desprairies, Cecile. *Ville Lumière, années noires: Les lieux de Paris de la Collaboration.* Paris: Denoël, 2008.

Diamond, Hanna. *Fleeing Hitler: France 1940.* New York: Oxford University Press, 2007.

Dumont, Jean. *Les grandes énigmes de l'Occupation. Tome 3.* Geneva: Ed. Crèmille, Beuval 1970.

Eberle, Henrik and Uhl, Matthias. *The Hitler Book.* London 2005.

Ellis, John; Cox, Michael. *The World War I Databook: The Essential Facts.* London: Aurum Press, 1993.

Fabré, Marc-André. *Dans les Prisons de Vichy.* Paris: A Michel, 1994.

Foot, M.R.D. *The Special Operations Executive 1940-1946.* London: London Bridge, 1999.

Foot, M.R.D. *SOE in France.* London: HMSO, 1968.

Freed, S. A. and R. S. "Origin of the Swastika", *Natural History, January* 1980, 68-75.

Gerhardt, Ute and Karlauf, Thomas. *The Night of the Broken Glass—Eyewitness Accounts of Kristallnacht.* Polity, UK, 2012.

Gildea, Robert. *Fighters in the Shadows: A New History of the French Resistance.* Faber & Faber, 2015.

Granet, Marie. *Les Jeunes de la Résistance en 1940.* Paris, 1985.

Grant, R.G. MI5, MI6: *Britain's Security and Secret Intelligence Services.* London, 1989.

Guilliaume, Paul. *La Sologne aux temps de l'heroisme et de la trahaison.* Orleans, 1950.

Hastings, Max. *Das Reich: The March of the 2nd SS Panzer Division Through France, June 1944.* Pan, 2012.

Hessel, Stéphane and Morin, Edgard. *Le Chemin de l'espèrance.* Fayard, Paris, 2011.

Hinsley, F.H. *British Intelligence in the Second World War,* five vols. London: HMSO, 1979-1990.

Hoare, Samuel S. *Ambassador on Special Mission.* London, 1946.

Jerome, Jean. *Les clandestines 1940-1944.* Paris, 1986.

Johnson, Kate, ed. *The Special Operations Executive:* Sound Archive—Oral History.

Jones, Liane. *A Quiet Courage.* London, 1990. *Recordings.* London, Imperial War Museum.

Kessel, Joseph. *L'armé des ombres.* Paris, 1963. Geneva, 1972.

Keward, H.R. *Occupied France, Collaboration and Resistance 1940-1944.* Oxford: Oxford University Press,1985.

Langelaan, George. *Knights of the Floating Silk.* London: Hutchinson, 1959

Ludewig, Joachim. *Rückzug: The German Retreat from France, 1944.* Lexington: University of Kentucky Press, 2012.

MacMillan, Margaret. *Paris 1919: Six Months That Changed the World.* London and New York: Random House, 2002.

Mackenzie, W.J.M. *The Secret History of SOE: The Special Operations Executive 1940-1945.* London: St. Ermin's Press, 2000 [1948].

Marks, Leo. *Between Silk and Cyanide- A Codemaker's War 1941-1945.* New York: Free Press, 1983.

Michal, Bernard with Bourget, Pierre. *Les grandes énigmes de la Résistance.* Paris: Les amis de l'Historie, 1968.

Moorehead, Caroline. *Village of Secrets: Defying the Nazis in Vichy France.* London: HarperCollins, 2014.

_____. *A Train in Winter: An Extraordinary Story of Women, Friendship and Resistance in Occupied France.* New York and London: HarperCollins, 2011.

Muchitsch, Wolfgang. *Österreicher im Exil—Grossbritannien 1938-1945. Eine Dokumentation.* Vienna: Österreichischer Bundesverlag, 1992.

Murphy, Dr. Christopher John. *Security and Special Operations*: SOE and *MI 5 during the Second World War*. Basingstoke: Palgrave Macmillan, 2006.

Noguères, Henri. *Histoire de la Résistance en France de 1940-1945*, five vols. Paris: Robert Laffont, 1967.

Novick, Peter. *The Resistance vs. Vichy: The Purge of Collaborators in Liberated France*. New York: Columbia University Press, 1958.

Paine, Lauran. *The Abwehr: German Military Intelligence in World War II*. London: Stein & Day, 1984.

Payne, Stanley G. *Franco and Hitler: Spain, Germany and World War II*. New Haven, CT: Yale University Press, 2008.

Perrin, Nigel. *Spirit of Resistance: The Life of SOE Agent Harry Peulevé, DSO. MC*. London: Pen and Sword, 2009.

Pidgeon, Geoffrey. *The Secret Wireless War: The Story of MI-6 Communications 1939-45*. Royal Turnbridge Wells, UK: Upso Ltd. 2007.

Piquet-Wicks, Eric. *Four in the Shadows: A True Story of Espionage in Occupied France*. London: Jarrolds, 1957.

Richards, Francis Brooks. *Secret Flotillas, Vol I—Clandestine Sea Operations to Brittany, 1940-1944*. London: Whitehall History Publishing, 2004.

Ruby, M. *F Section, SOE: The Buckmaster Networks*. London: Leo Cooper, 1990.

Schuschnigg, Kurt. *The Brutal Takeover: The Austrian ex-Chancellor's Account of the Anschluss of Austria by Hitler*. London: Atheneum, 1971.

Seaman, Mark. *Special Operations Executive: A New Instrument of War*. London: Routledge 2006.

SOE Syllabus: Lessons in Ungentlemanly Warfare, World War II.
London: The National Archives, 2004.

Stafford, David. *Britain and European Resistance, 1940-1945:*
A Survey of the Special Operations Executive. Toronto, 1980.

_____. *Churchill and the Secret Service.* New York 1997.

Terrisse, René. *Grandclément: Traître ou bouc-émissaire?* Paris:
Aubéron, 1996.

Verity, Hugh. *We Landed by Moonlight: Secret RAF Landings in*
France 1940-1945. Manchester, UK: Crecy Publishing, 1998.

Vance, Jonathan F. *Unlikely Soldiers: How Two Canadians Fought*
the Secret War against Nazi Occupation. Toronto: Harper
Collins, 2008.

Vinen, Richard. *The Unfree French: Life Under the Occupation.* New
Haven, CT: Yale University Press, 2006.

Vomécourt, Philippe de. *Who Lived to See the Day: France in Arms,*
1940-1945. London: Hutchinson, 1961.

Waller, John H. *The Unseen War in Europe: Espionage and Conspiracy*
in the Second World War. New York and London: I.B. Tauris, 1996.

Wieviorka, Olivier. *Histoire de la Résistance, 1940-1945—Obéir, c'est*
trahir. Désobéir, c'est server. Paris, Editions: Perrin, 2013.

External links/websites

The Special Operations Executive (Official Document—British
Foreign & Commonwealth Office Website).

Profiles of Special Operations Executive Agents in France at Nigel
Perrin's website.

Colin Gubbins, Leo Marks and the SOE.

Imperial War Museum (London) IWM Secret War exhibition.

Imperial War Museum Collections Online IWM Collections Irregular Warfare, for many written materials, photos, audio files on SOE.

"Mission Scapula" Special Operations Executive in the Far East.

Target near Glasnacardoch Lodge STS22a.

The Violette Szabo Museum.

64 Baker Street, the women of the SOE.

Canadian Secret Agents in the Second World War.

Operation BRADDOCK—A joint SOE/PWE plan to air-drop concealable explosive devices across Europe.

Roll of honour, awards and images.

SOE sites around Milton Keynes.
The 11th Day Documentary film about the Resistance, on the island of Crete, during the Second World War including SOE efforts and Sir Patrick Leigh Fermor.

Gladiators of World War II—Episode 2, Special Operations Executive. Available on YouTube.

Interview with secret agent Francis Cammaerts in the Leicester Mercury.

"Para-Military Training in Scotland during World War 2". Land, Sea & Islands Centre. 2001. An account of SOE training around the Arisaig.

http://www.tempsford-squadrons.info/

http://www.161squadron.org/

http://www.plan-sussex-1944.net

FILMOGRAPHY

Now It Can Be Told (aka *School for Danger*) (1946).Filming began in 1944 and starred real-life SOE agents Captain Harry Rée and Jacqueline Nearne. The film tells the story of the training of agents for SOE and their adventures in France. The training sequences were filmed using the SOE equipment at the training schools at Traigh and Garramor (South Morar) and at Ringway.

The Fight over the Heavy Water (1948). A French/Norwegian black and white docu-film titled "La Bataille de l'eau lourde"/"Kampen om tungtvannet" (trans. "The Fight Over Heavy Water"), featured some of the 'original cast', so to speak. Joachim Rønneberg has stated; "The Fight over Heavy Water was an honest attempt to describe history. On the other hand 'Heroes of Telemark' had little to do with reality."

- *Odette* (1950). Based on the book by Jerrard Tickell about Odette Sansom, starring Anna Neagle and Trevor Howard. The film includes an interview with Maurice Buckmaster, head of F-Section, SOE.

- *Ill Met by Moonlight* (film) (1957). Powell and Pressburger film, (released as *Night Ambush* in the United States), based on the book by Patrick Leigh Fermor & W. Stanley Moss, starring Dirk Bogarde and Marius Goring. It dramatises the true story of the capture of a German general.

- *Carve Her Name with Pride* (1958). Based on the book by R.J. Minney about Violette Szabo, starring Paul Scofield and Virginia McKenna.

- *The Guns of Navarone* (1961). Based on a well-known 1957 novel about the Second World War by Alistair MacLean, the film starred Gregory Peck, David Niven and Anthony Quinn, along with Anthony Quayle (the same Anthony Quayle who served with the SOE in Albania). The book and the film feature the efforts of an Allied commando team to destroy an impregnable German fortress that threatens Allied naval shipping in the Aegean Sea, and prevents 2,000 isolated British troops that were holed up on the island of Kheros from being rescued.

- *Moonstrike* (1963). A BBC television drama series comprised of self-contained episodes relating to the SOE's work in occupied Europe.

- *The Heroes of Telemark* (1965). Film based on an SOE operation to sabotage the heavy water plant at Rjukan, Norway in 1943.

- *Operation Crossbow* (1965). A Second World War spy thriller inspired by a story by Duilio Coletti and Vittoriano Petrilli. A highly fictionalised account of the real-life Operation Crossbow and fails to touch on the main aspects of the operation.

- *Where Eagles Dare* (1968). A spy film directed by Brian G. Hutton and featuring Richard Burton, Clint Eastwood, and Mary Ure. The film's 1957 screenplay and best-selling novel were written almost simultaneously by Alistair MacLean.

- *Operation Daybreak* (1976). Based on a true, dangerous operation in May 1942 to drop a small group of Czech and Slovak SOE agents into their own Nazi-occupied country to assassinate SS Reichsführer Heinrich Himmler's protégé, Reinhard Heydrich—later villified as 'The Butcher of Prague'.

- *Au revoir les enfants* (<u>1987</u>) is a classic autobiographical film written, produced and directed by Louis Malle. The screenplay was published by Gallimard the same year. The film also won the Golden Lion award at the Venice Film Festival.

- *Nancy Wake, Codename: The White Mouse* (1987). A docudrama about Wake's work for SOE, narrated in part by Nancy Wake herself.

- *Wish Me Luck* (1987). A television series broadcast between 1987 and 1990 featuring the exploits of the women and, less frequently, the men of SOE, which was renamed the 'Outfit'.

- *Charlotte Gray* (2001). Based on a novel by Sebastian Faulks.

- *Churchill's Secret Army* (2000). A three-part documentary series about the SOE originally broadcast by the BBC.

- *Jean Moulin—Une affaire française* (2004). Film made for television. Directed by Pierre Aknine. Scarlett Productions. Foyle's War Episode: "The French Drop" (2004). Detective Inspector

Foyle investigates what turns out to be domestic activity on the part of the SOE. The series is known for its attention to historical detail and many true-to-life aspects of the SOE are included.

- *Robert and the Shadows* (2004). French documentary on "France Television." Did General De Gaulle tell the whole truth about the French resistance ? The quest for the answer is the purpose that drives this documentary. Jean Marie Barrere, the director, uses the story of his own grandfather, Robert, to reveal the role played by the SOE at that time. Robert, was a teacher based in the south west of France and worked with the famous SOE agent George Reginald Starr. (Hilaire, Wheelwright circuit).

- *The 11th Day* (2006). A documentary film featuring the Resistance on the island of Crete, during the Second World War. It includes a detailed interview with former agent Sir Patrick Leigh Fermor and recreates the kidnapping of German Major General Kreipe.

- *The Bonzos* (2008). A BBC documentary film about the men sent to rescue Hitler's hoard of looted art—including works by Titian, Tintoretto and Van Gogh—which the Nazis had stripped from Europe's greatest galleries and museums and hidden in a salt mine in Austria. Archival footage, eyewitness testimony and contributions from historians feature prominently.

- *Churchill's Spy School* (2010). A documentary about the SOE "finishing school" on the Beaulieu estate in Hampshire

- *Les Femmes de l'Ombre* (2011). A French film about five SOE female agents and their contribution towards the D-Day invasion. Jean-Paul Salomé, the director, drew inspiration from an obituary in *The Times* about Lise de Baissac, one of the organisation's few recognised heroines.

- *Age of Heroes* (2011). A film about the formation of a Special Operations team and their mission to destroy Nazi radar equipment in Norway during the Second World War.

ADDENDUM

A substantial number of detailed entries in Pierre Tillet's 2014 work-in-progress—*A Tentative History of In/Exfiltrations into/from France during WWII from 1940 to 1945 (Parachutes, Plane & Sea Landings)*—continue until 17 November 1944. Countless Allied operations involving many different agencies are meticulously documented for referral. However, following the ultimate success of the D-Day landings on June 6th 1944 and the subsequent Liberation of Paris on 25 August 1944, it became clear that further documentation of each of these extensive operations was well beyond the scope of my original intention.

On the other hand, the documentation provided by m. Tillet vividly points up the slow but determined advance of the covert 'Army of Shadows' in France aligned against the increasingly oppressive Nazi Occupation between 1941 and 1945. The details of each 'operation' are individually recorded not merely as impressive statistical data, but as a testament to the exemplary courage displayed by those committed to the work of the French Resistance and by Special Operations agents. Undaunted by the ever-present prospect of betrayal, capture, imprisonment, unspeakable torture and probable execution at the hands of an enemy determined to bring them to their knees, they persevered against unimaginable odds.

As well, all too often—as these operational records demonstrate—the extent to which these men and women were prepared to put their lives on the line in the name of freedom from oppression is there for all to see. The number of aircraft lost—not only to enemy fire, but to engine failure, foul weather, crash landings, and just plain rotten luck—is staggering. And at sea, all manner of vessels from submarines to fishing boats and high-speed MTBs were constantly facing the spectre of disaster as they went about the business of infiltration and rescue.

Who can read these records without experiencing a sense of incalculable wonder at the extent of individual preparedness to risk everything and—if necessary—pay the ultimate price without regret?

---

* Interested readers may follow the entire body of research undertaken by m. Tillet online in either French of English at pierre.tillet@free.fr or infiltrations_into_france.pdf.

END NOTES

Chapter 1

1. Canadian scholar and historian Margaret Macmillan's book *Paris 1919— Six Months That Changed the World* which was published to great critical acclaim on the subject of the Versailles Peace Treaty has been widely regarded as the seminal work on this brief but crucial period in the history of the 20th century. Macmillan's great-grandfather, Lloyd George would undoubtedly have been well pleased with this stellar contribution to accounts of this crucial post-WWI milestone.

2. John Ellis and Michael Cox's *The World War I Databook* provides a comprehensive source of information relating to all areas of the conflict and includes statistics on all the military forces deployed as well as the casualties and losses. For France, the casualty figures total almost one and a half million killed and over four million wounded.

3. Bluche, François. *L'Ancien Régime: Institutions et société*. Collection: Livre de poche. Paris, 1993.

4. Excerpt from Robert De La Rochefoucauld's memoir: *La liberté, C'est mon plaisir*. Paris, 2002.

5. Ibid.

6. Marist Fathers—A religious order of priests established in Rouen, France circa 1816. Its adherents professed a particular devotion to the Order's namesake, the Blessed Virgin.

Chapter Two

1. According to a description in the 2005 publication, *The Hitler Book* by Henrik Eberle and Matthias Uhl, the original chalet situated in close proximity to the town of Bertchesgaden in the Southern Bavaria Alps, was refurbished and renovated in 1935 for Adolf Hitler's personal use. It then became known as the Berghof or Eagle's Nest and was unquestionably Hitler's favoured location for relaxation and entertaining—most likely due to its proximity to his native Austria and also because of its spectacular vantage point. In May 1945, the Berghof was bombed by the Allies and later seized by French occupying forces and subsequently the US military.

2. Excerpt from Robert De La Rochefoucauld's memoir : *La liberté, C'est mon plaisir.* Paris, 2002.

3. "Origin of the Swastika" a description of the ancient sign of the swastika compiled by S. A. and R. S Freed for the *Natural History* journal in January 1980, pp. 68-75.

4. In his semi-autobiographical treatise *Mein Kampf* published in 1925, Adolf Hitler describes the significance of the emblem he had personally chosen to represent the NationalSocialist Party "In red we see the social idea of the movement, in white the nationalistic characteristics of the Aryan man…"

5. Within one week of the annexation of Austria, on March 12, 1938, Hitler had dispatched two of his most highly prized henchmen, Heinrich Himmler and Reinhard Heydrich, to orchestrate and oversee the systematic "cleansing" of Vienna's substantial Jewish population along with "other undesirables."

6. Schuschnigg, Kurt. *The Brutal Takeover: The Austrian ex-Chancellor's Account of the Anschluss of Austria by Hitler.* London, Weidenfeld and Nicolson, 1971.

7. Excerpt from Robert De La Rochefoucauld's memoir: *La liberté, C'est mon plaisir.* Paris, 2002.

8. The Sigmund Freud Museum, Vienna.

9. Von Trapp, Maria. *The Story of the Trapp Family Singers.* New York, 1949.

10. *The Night of the Broken Glass—Eyewitness Accounts of Kristallnacht* by Uta Gerhardt and Thomas Karlauf. These accounts include chilling first-hand reportage of the countless despicable acts perpetrated against Jewish citizens, synagogues and businesses throughout Germany on "The Night of Shattered Glass," November 9/10 , 1938.

11. The so-called Phoney War of 1939-1940 was also referred to by Winston Churchill as "The Twilight War" in the sense that between 3 September 1939 and early May 1940, virtually no major military activity took place between the main protagonists—France, Britain and Germany.

12. A total of 338,226 combatants (198,229 British and 139,997 French) were rescued from the beaches of Dunkirk by a hastily assembled fleet of 933 vessels.

13. Excerpt from Robert De La Rochefoucauld's memoir: *La liberté, C'est mon plaisir.* Paris, 2002.

14. Moorehead, Caroline, *A Train in Winter: An Extraordinary Story of Women, Friendship and Resistance in Occupied France.* New York and London, 2011.

15. Excerpt from Robert De La Rochefoucauld's memoir: *La liberté, C'est mon plaisir.* Paris, 2002.

16. It was common knowledge in France, if not elsewhere, that on 2 August, 1940, General de Gaulle had been sentenced to death in an absentia by a military tribunal established by Pétain's Vichy regime.

17. Excerpt from Robert De La Rochefoucauld's memoir: *La liberté, C'est mon plaisir.* Paris, 2002

18. Dallek, David, *Franklin D. Roosevelt and American Foreign Policy. 1932-1945.* Oxford, 1979, p.256.

Chapter Three

1. Etienne Archavanne was the first French citizen to be captured, tried and executed on 6 July, 1940 by the Germany Occupying Forces for committing a deliberate act of sabotage, thus becoming the first martyr of the Resistance. Wieviorka, Olivier. *Histoire de la Résistance, 1940-1945*, p.13.

2. Ibid, p.33.

3. Vomécourt, Philippe de. *Who Lived to See the Day: France in Arms, 1940-1945.* London, 1961, p.26.

4. Excerpt from Robert De La Rochefoucauld's memoir: *La liberté, C'est mon plaisir.* Paris, 2002.

5. Ibid.

6. Perpignan is the southern-most city of the Longuedoc region which borders

Spain and as such became a major destination for the French Underground's escape network during WW II.

7.   Originally produced in 1969, the classic film *Army of Shadows* was recently re-issued and provides a riveting insight into the workings of the World War II Resistance movement in France. It is an adaptation of Joseph Kessel's 1943 book of the same name, which incorporates Kessel's own experiences as a member of the Underground.

8.   Excerpt from Robert De La Rochefoucauld's memoir: *La liberté, C'est mon plaisir*. Paris, 2002.

9.   An entire chapter in Philippe de Vomécourt's *Who Lived to See the Day: France in Arms, 1940-1945*, p. 49–56 is devoted to the emergence of the clandestine escape routes set up to smuggle European refugees as well as Allied airmen and agents out of France and across the Pyrenees into Spain.

Chapter Four

1.   Official statistics reveal that between 1940 and 1944 there were roughly 33,000 escapees from Occupied France who managed to make their way across one of several arduous routes through the Pyrenees—the chain of mountains which separates Southwestern France and Spain. According to Scott Goodall's 85 page guide, *Le Chemin de la Liberté*, since early 1943, German losses prompted increased surveillance along the French—Spanish border. Border patrols in Vichy France were reinforced and betrayals encouraged. This led to a substantial number of ambushes along the various escape routes, where a total of over a hundred guides known as passeurs were either arrested and deported or shot on sight.

2.   Excerpt from Robert De La Rochefoucauld's memoir: *La liberté, C'est mon plaisir*. Paris, 2002.

3.   The city of Miranda del Ebro in northeastern Spain was the site of one of the largest and most notorious of General Francisco Franco's numerous prisons and was designated primarily for the incarceration of political prisoners—both domestic and foreign.

4.   Eric Picquet-Wicks' book, *Four in the Shadows: A True Story of Espionage in Occupied France* relating to his wartime role in the British Special Operations and the activities of its secret agents was published in London in 1957.

5.   With the advance of Nazi invasion and occupation, in less than a year, Berne and Lisbon, which had previously been the centres of British Intelligence on the Continent, were displaced by Madrid due to its strategic location. The

city had also become central to furthering British interests—including un-dercover activities. From 1940 to 1944 Samuel S. Hoare—later 1st Viscount of Templewood and a veteran diplomat—rendered invaluable service as the British ambassador to Madrid, and provided assistance to countless num-bers of refugees from war torn Europe. His memoirs entitled *Ambassador on Special Mission* were published in London in 1946.

6. Excerpt from Robert De La Rochefoucauld's memoir: *La liberté, C'est mon plaisir*. Paris, 2002.

Chapter Five

1. From early 1943 onwards, Allied bombing raids over targets in Germany greatly intensified. These included the remarkably successful " Dambusters" raid as well as 'Operation Bellicose' which was the first attack aimed at the destruction of a V-2 rocket site located at the Zeppelin factory in Friederichshafen. However, these missions over enemy territory all came at an enormous price as thousands of aircrew made the ultimate sacrifice in the struggle to bring down Hitler's Third Reich.

2. Excerpt from Robert De La Rochefoucauld's memoir: *La liberté, C'est mon plaisir*. Paris, 2002.

3. The Special Operations Executive or SOE was also referred to as " Churchill's Secret Army", as well as by several other clever sobriquets such as " The Baker Street Irregulars"—after the address of its London Headquarters—or possibly in memory of Sherlock Holmes's fictional group of spies. Among a number of other colourful nicknames, it was referred to as "The Ministry of Ungentlemanly Warfare". Between mid-1940 and 1945, the various departments and agencies of the SOE comprised over 13,000 men and women—all of whom were required to sign the Official Secrets Act and were effectively sworn to silence about their wartime activities for the better part of a lifetime. In fact a good many of these brave men and women died with their secrets unrevealed.

4. General de Gaulle's inaugural broadcast from London was transmitted by the BBC to legions of listeners in France on 18 June, 1940—little more than a month after the Nazi Swastika was first raised over German-occupied Paris. The following is a partial translation of this historic message—the same stirring message of inspiration that left its indelible mark on the teen-aged patriot of Chateaux Villeneuve, Robert De La Rochefoucauld:

> The French government, after having asked for an armistice, now knows the conditions dictated by the enemy.

The result of these conditions would be the complete demobilisation of the French land, sea, and air forces, the surrender of our weapons and the total occupation of French territory. The French government would come under German and Italian tutelage.

It may therefore be said that this armistice would not only be a capitulation, but that it would also reduce the country to slavery. Now, a great many Frenchmen refuse to accept either capitulation or slavery, for reasons which are called: honour, common sense, and the higher interests of the country.

I say honour, for France has undertaken not to lay down arms save in agreement with her allies. As long as the allies continue the war, her government has no right to surrender to the enemy. The Polish, Norwegian, Belgian, Netherlands, and Luxemburg governments, though driven from their territories, have thus interpreted their duty.

I say common sense, for it is absurd to consider the struggle as lost. True, we have suffered a major defeat. We lost the battle of France through a faulty military system, mistakes in the conduct of operations, and the defeatist spirit shown by the government during recent battles....

I say the higher interests of the country, for this is not a Franco-German war to be decided by a single battle. This is a world war. No one can foresee whether the neutral countries of today will not be at war tomorrow, or whether Germany's allies will always remain her allies. If the powers of freedom ultimately triumph over those of servitude, what will be the fate of a France which has submitted to the enemy?

Honour, common sense, and the interests of the country require that all free Frenchmen, wherever they may be, should continue the fight as best they can...

I, General de Gaulle, am undertaking this national task here in England.

I call upon all French servicemen of the land, sea, and air forces; I call upon French engineers and skilled armaments workers who are on British soil, or have the means of getting here, to come and join me.... I call upon all Frenchmen who want to remain free to listen to my voice and follow me.

Long live Free France in honour and independence!"

5.   French diplomat, Geoffroy Chodron de Courcel (1912–1992) was aide-de-camp to General Charles de Gaulle in 1940 and escaped to England with the General on 17 June 1940. When de Gaulle established the Free French Forces in London, de Courcel was the first officer enlisted. In 1941, in addition to his position as Aide-de-camp, he became de Gaulle's principal private secretary. After the war, he returned to the French Foreign Ministry and held a number of important appointments including that of Ambassador to the United Kingdom from March 1962 until April 1972.

6.   Excerpt from Robert De La Rochefoucauld's memoir : *La liberté, C'est mon plaisir.* Paris, 2002.

7.   Ibid.

8.   Following his brief but decisive meeting with de Gaulle in London late in 1942, LaRochefoucauld adds the following humorous anecdote which appeared in his 2002 memoir:

> I never again saw General de Gaulle during the War, but much later I was his invited guest at a special reception at the Élysée Palace in Paris. Unfortunately I did not have the opportunity to speak with him on that occasion. I remember only that protocol required guests of the President of the Republic to be chauffeur-driven to the Presidential Palace. To accomplish this, I conscripted my younger brother, Aymeri, to be my chauffeur for the evening. He parked expertly at the foot of the front steps, however the car chose that precise moment to break down and stubbornly refused to start up again! An impossible situation made worse by the fact that it was equally impossible to leave the car blocking access to other vehicles entering the courtyard. Our only recourse was to push the car as far away from the scene of our embarrassment as possible with the help of the Republican Guard. A memorable occasion, indeed.

9.   Men and women who were agents under the aegis of the Special Operations Executive were among those trained to jump at the Royal Air Force station located at Ringwood on the outskirts of Manchester. From June 1940 onwards Ringwood became the wartime base for No.1 Parachute Training School RAF, which was charged with the initial training of all allied paratroopers trained in Europe (60,000). It was here that techniques for parachute drops of equipment were also developed as well as military gliding operations.

10. Excerpt from Robert De La Rochefoucauld's memoir : *La liberté, C'est mon plaisir.* Paris, 2002.

11.   According to the Home Security Situation Report to the War Office for the week ending 30th December 1942, there was no military purpose behind these so-called 'nuisance raids'. The Blitz had completely failed to bomb the British into submission and as a result further attacks against civilians were now merely for the purpose of harassment. These minor 'nuisance' raids, which could prove devastating to local communities, were a continuation of the larger 'Baedeker raids' which had targeted specific towns noted for their historical significance.

Chapter Six

1.   The initial aspect of every agent's training involved various tests and a subsequent assessment of his or her character and potential, without revealing too many details about precisely what was entailed. Those candidates earmarked as unsuitable were soon sent to the 'cooler', where they were encouraged to forget the little they had learned about the SOE, while those who passed the preliminary stage were sent to paramilitary schools, known as the Group A schools.

       The precise location of the initial training phase undergone by De La Rochefoucauld remains unknown. It is entirely possible that more than a few SOE trainees had no knowledge of exactly where they had been taken to complete the various phases in their preparation for active duty behind enemy lines. Once concluded, however, they were doubtless well aware of their vastly increased knowledge, physical stamina and powers of endurance. One of the best known of these secluded Group A sites and one which specialized in commando-style training—was situated somewhere in the far reaches of the Scottish Highlands at Arisaig House in Inverness-shire.

       This particular phase of De La Rochefoucauld's training, i.e. the skills required to become proficient as a paratrooper, would have been completed at RAF Station Ringway, now the location of Manchester Airport. (See Chapter 5—End Note 8)

2.   Excerpt from Robert De La Rochefoucauld's memoir : *La liberté, C'est mon plaisir.* Paris 2002.

3.   The Fairbairn–Sykes combat knife is a double-edged weapon resembling a dagger with a foil grip developed by its namesakes: William Ewart Fairbairn and Eric Anthony Sykes in Shanghai. They had based the design on concepts which the two men utilized prior to World War II while serving on the Shanghai Municipal Police. The Fairbairn–Sykes knife achieved its reputation during World War II when it was issued to British Commandos, the Airborne Forces, and numerous other fighting units, especially in

preparation for the Normandy Landings in June 1944. With its razor-sharp tapered blade, the Fairbairn–Sykes combat knife is frequently described as a stiletto, an ideal weapon for thrusting, although the knife could also be effective when used to inflict slash-wounds on an opponent. The Wilkinson Sword Company made the knife with minor pommel and grip design variations.

4. Excerpt from Robert De La Rochefoucauld's memoir : *La liberté, C'est mon plaisir.* Paris, 2002.

5. Although the specific locale for his instruction in the intricacies of interrogation is not mentioned in De La Rochefoucauld's memoir, most probably this took place at Beaulieu Abbey, which was the largest of several top-secret SOE stations situated on the grounds of various secluded estates and manor houses in the English countryside. This gave rise to yet another of the terms of reference for the letters SOE, namely "Stately 'Omes of England". In the case of Beaulieu, the element of secrecy was considered so crucial that the very existence of this training school had to be kept from the local community. In fact, the degree of secrecy even extended to the members of the Montague family, whose house was in the middle of the complex. It is purported that they, too, were completely unaware of what was actually taking place in their midst. *Beaulieu: The Finishing School for Secret Agents* by Cyril Cunningham.

6. John Pearson's 1967 biography, *The Life of Ian Fleming: Creator of James Bond* published three years after Fleming's death provides interesting insights into the role Commander Fleming played in numerous wartime operations, as well as his involvement with MI-6 and the SOE.

7. Excerpt from Robert De La Rochefoucauld's memoir: *La liberté, C'est mon plaisir.* Paris, 2002.

8. Ibid.

Chapter Seven

1. Initially SOE agents were given clothes that had been acquired from European refugees to Britain, however supplies soon ran short of demand. It was at this stage that the SOE 'support section' came up with its own camouflage department which specialised in the production of apparel that exactly replicated continental patterns. The degree of minutia involved even extended to the type of stitching used on each garment or shoe style. Every article of clothing and accessory had to be indistinguishable from the genuine article to ensure that there would be no tell-tale signs of their true origin.

2.   RAF Tempsford was perhaps the most secret airfield in World War II. It was home to the Special Duties Squadrons, No. 138, which dropped Special Operations Executive (SOE) agents and their supplies into occupied Europe, and No. 161, which specialised in personnel delivery and retrieval by landing in occupied Europe.

3.   Frequently the aircraft used for the execution of these drops was either the indomitable Douglas C-47 Dakota—a military transport aircraft—which was without doubt one of the most successful aircraft designs in aviation history. The smaller twin-engine A.W.38 Whitley Mark V was also used for the same purpose due to the aircraft's good takeoff and landing performance.

4.   Excerpt from Robert De La Rochefoucauld's memoir: *La liberté, C'est mon plaisir.* Paris, 2002.

5.   Originally the word *maquis* was derived from the remote and inaccessible terrain of south eastern France in which armed resistance groups were best able to avoid detection. Much of the region is covered with scrub growth known as maquis or thickets which, in turn, provided the maquisards with excellent cover.

        Although the Maquis used whatever arms they could get their hands on, they heavily relied on airdrops of weapons and explosives from the British SOE, which parachuted in containers with various munitions including Sten guns, pencil detonators, plastic explosives, Welrod pistols (a silenced specialized assassination weapon favored by covert operatives) and assorted small arms (pistols, rifles and sub-machine guns. The Maquis also used German weapons captured throughout the Occupation, such the Mauser 98k rifle and MP 40 submachine gun.

6.   Avallon is located 50 km south-southeast of Auxerre in east-central France. The old town, with many winding cobblestone streets flanked by traditional stone and timbered buildings, is situated on a flat promontory, the base of which abuts the Cousin River on the south and small streams on the east and west.

7.   Excerpt from Robert De La Rochefoucauld's memoir: *La liberté, C'est mon plaisir.* Paris, 2002.

8.   Ibid.

9.   The Milice française (French Militia)—generally known simply as the Milice—was a paramilitary force created on January 30, 1943 by the Vichy Regime, with full German collaboration, to help counteract the work of the French Resistance. It participated in summary executions and assassinations and helped round up Jews and résistants in France for deportation.

The Milice frequently resorted to torture to extract information or confessions from those whom they rounded up. Certain members of the French Resistance actually considered the Milice to be more dangerous than either the Gestapo and the SS because its membership was almost exclusively French with extensive knowledge of the towns and local countryside, and of those who collaborated with them as informers. Olivier Wieviorka, *Histoire de la Resistance*. Paris, 2013.

Chapter Eight

1. There is a permanent exhibition mounted at the Musée Jean Moulin in Paris established in honour of this revered French patriot. As well, SOE's Eric Piquet-Wickes, who knew and greatly admired Moulin, highlights his life and accomplishments in his book *Four in the Shadows* (1957) and honours his invaluable contribution to the French Resistance until his death by torture in June 1943.

2. The origins of the city of Auxerre date back to a Roman settlement on the banks of the Yonne River in Burgundy. According to local historians, in the tenth century the local wolf packs were so large and vicious, that they forced the Dukes of Burgundy from their capital in Auxerre to the safer regions of Dijon. During World War II, with a dearth of men in the city due to the absence of those taken as prisoners of war in 1940 or sent by the Occupation Forces for forced labor in Germany, there was little to be done when wolves once more reappeared in the region. At one point, a pack of starving wolves that had consumed one too many grapes ran into the center of the city and lay down in a drunken stupor. According to an eye-witness "The wolves were all intoxicated... they were too drunk to remember they were wolves." The sight prompted the frightened townspeople of Auxerre to emerge with their kitchen knives and put the wolves out of their misery.

3. Excerpt from Robert De La Rochefoucauld's memoir: *La liberté, C'est mon plaisir.* Paris, 2002.

4. Ibid.

5. Ibid.

6. Ibid.

7. From 1940 onwards, anonymous individuals within France who were without any affiliation to the Resistance can be credited for having saved countless lives, including those of thousands of Jews, Allied agents and downed airmen, all of whom were on the run from the Nazi oppressors and the

dreaded Milice. Translated from p. 497 in Olivier Wieviorka's 2013 *Histoire de la Résistance: Obéir c'est trahir. Désobéir, c'est servir.* [*To obey is a betrayal. To disobey is to serve*]

8. Excerpt from Robert De La Rochefoucauld's memoir: *La liberté, C'est mon plaisir.* Paris, 2002.

9. Ibid.

Chapter Nine

1. Excerpt from Robert De La Rochefoucauld's memoir: *La liberté, C'est mon plaisir.* Paris, 2002.

2. The Service du Travail Obligatoire, or STO, a Nazi requirement, was imposed in 1942 and vigorously enforced by the Vichy government under Pierre Laval. He was later tried for treason as a collaborator and executed. Essentially, the imposition of this enforced labour requirement was to provide a supplemental labour force for a beleaguered Germany and it applied universally to all young Frenchmen unless they could prove they were 'legitimately' exempt.

3. Excerpt from Robert De La Rochefoucauld's memoir: *La liberté, C'est mon plaisir.* Paris, 2002.

4. Ibid.

5. Situated on France's Opal Coast, Berck is renowned for its huge expanse of sandy beach and impressive grass-topped dunes facing north onto the English Channel. The town is comprised of two parts—to the east, the historic fishing town of Berck-Ville and to the west the seaside resort area, Berck-sur-Mer. In the 19th century, the area became a popular destination for Parisian painters such as Edouard Manet, who were attracted by the dunes and the unique light. It was also long frequented by tubercular patients and others in need of its bracing air.

6. Excerpt from Robert De La Rochefoucauld's memoir: *La liberté, C'est mon plaisir.* Paris, 2002.

Chapter Ten

1. The Resistance relied on coded messages to communicate and to plan operations. Members were called by code names, and operational units had their own cryptonym or symbols. Underground newspapers published coded articles and drawings. Poetry was even used as a means of sending

coded messages or identifying oneself as a member of a Resistance group to other members.

2.   Excerpt from Robert De La Rochefoucauld's memoir: *La liberté, C'est mon plaisir.* Paris, 2002.

3.   Ibid.

4.   An examination into the life and death in 1944 of perceived traitor, André Grandclément, is documented by René Terrisse in his 1996 publication : *Grandclément, traître ou bouc-émissaire?*

5.   Excerpt from Robert De La Rochefoucauld's memoir: *La liberté, C'est mon plaisir.* Paris, 2002.

Chapter Eleven

1.   In June 1944, roughly a hundred teams of uniformed Jedburgh commando units collaborated with clandestine networks throughout Europe to inflict as much damage as possible on enemy transport, supplies, and morale. Working in groups of three, they also coordinated the procurement and allocation of radios to facilitate their operations. While the use of radios carried an increased risk of detection by the enemy, they had the advantage of enabling communication over greater distances. According to SOE code-master, Leo Marks, messages were transmitted nightly, both to Allied command and to various partisan groups. These transmissions—which were never to be more than two hundred letters in length—identified their recipients with a cryptonym.

The codes themselves were agreed upon in person, and then used to activate plans as required. The result was that—if intercepted—the meanings of the messages were literally impossible to decipher. Although the method was basically primitive, nonetheless it proved effective as it left the Germans with only one possibility. They would have to rely on questionably reliable infiltrators as a means of discovering details relating to possible acts of sabotage on the part of the various Resistance networks.

2.   The Resistance network operating in the Bordeaux region in May 1944 bore the code-name ACTOR. Its leader, Roger Landes, had parachuted into the region three months earlier to consolidate activities in the Gironde. Presumably the group known as Bayard was part of this newly established network. Michael D. R. Foote's *SOE in France*, p. 360. Revised edition 2004.

3.   Excerpt from Robert De La Rochefoucauld's memoir: *La liberté, C'est mon plaisir.* Paris, 2002.

4.   'Bayard' was the *nom de guerre* of colourful French Resistance leader, Marcel Descour, (1899—1995) who co-ordinated many successful sabotage operations in the Gironde region—including *Operation Soleil. The Independent,* 13 May, 1995.

5.   Plastic or plastique is a specialised form of explosive material which is both supple and malleable and therefore also referred to as ' putty '. One of the simplest plastic explosives was Nobel's Explosive No. 808 developed by the British company Nobel Chemicals Ltd well before World War II. It had the appearance of green plasticine and the distinctive smell of almonds. During World War II it was used extensively by the British Special Operations Executive (SOE) for sabotage missions. It is even rumoured that SOE-supplied Nobel 808 was the explosive used in the failed 20 July assassination attempt on Adolf Hitler in 1944.

6.   Excerpt from Robert De La Rochefoucauld's memoir: *La liberté, C'est mon plaisir.* Paris, 2002.

7.   Ibid.

8.   Ibid

Chapter Twelve

1.   During their Occupation of France, the Nazis used the historic 15th century fortress of Hâ close to the Cathedral in Bordeaux for the confinement of so-called political prisoners including captured members of the Resistance as well anyone regarded as remotely 'uncooperative'. This would include those who had been discovered making 'illegal ' use of a radio by tuning in or listening to broadcasts on forbidden frequencies. *The fortress has since been levelled and the space is now occupied by the College of Magistrates. M. R. Bordes. *La Vie au fort du Hâ sous l'occupation.* éditions Bière, 1945.

2.   Information issued by the International Spy Museum in Washington D.C. notes that the SOE evidently issued potassium cyanide crystals—also known as the L- pill (L for lethal)—to field agents on high-risk missions which might result in capture and interrogation. Upon ingestion, the effects of this fast-acting poison would induce death within three to five minutes or less.

3.   The prospects for an intelligence operative captured by enemy forces were grim. Uniformed combatants had recourse to Geneva Convention

protocols concerning treatment, but personnel working in intelligence and covert operations were effectively denied such protection by virtue of their mission's clandestine nature.

During WWII imprisonment was likely to include lengthy exposure to coercive methods, including beatings and/or torture whose intention was to induce the operative to divulge sensitive information. For some, the risk seemed too great, and therefore field agents often embarked on dangerous missions equipped with the L-pill—a deadly compound of nitrogen, carbon, and other elements known as cyanide. Judson Knight. *The Encyclopaedia of Espionage.*

4.   Excerpt from Robert De La Rochefoucauld's memoir: *La liberté, C'est mon plaisir.* Paris, 2002.

5.   The Communists blamed for the 'Operation Soleil ' sabotage on the munitions plant at Saint-Médard-en-Jalles near Bordeaux were almost certainly among those denounced by local Resistance leader, André Grandclement, who was persuaded by the German authorities that his co-operation would be rendering a great service to post-war France.

6.   Excerpt from Robert De La Rochefoucauld's memoir: *La liberté, C'est mon plaisir.* Paris, 2002.

7.   An obituary notice for Major Roger Landes MC age 91 appeared in the July 29/2013 edition of the Telegraph. His *nom de guerre* was 'Aristide'.

"Landes had been sent back to Bordeaux in March 1944 to rebuild the local network in time for D-Day, a task that he knew could not be accomplished without first dealing with the treacherous Grandclément and his wife. Consequently, the couple were swiftly captured by the Resistance and persuaded that they were to be flown to England, where they would be able to argue their case. They were taken to the supposed landing site to wait for the aircraft that they were told would be taking them to England. Once there, Landes told Grandclément that he would have to be separated from his wife for security reasons. As Grandclément walked ahead, one of the other Resistance members shot him in the back of the head. At the same time, Landes pressed his pistol to the back of Mme Grandclément's head and killed her.

After the war Landes discovered from a former Gestapo officer that Mme Grandclément had opposed her husband's involvement with the Germans. But he still believed her death to be unavoidable. "We were discussing with the other men from the Maquis who was going to kill the woman," Landes later said. "Being in charge of the group, it was my duty to do it. We couldn't let her go, you see, because if I had been arrested, my entire group would have been in jeopardy. I was responsible for the lives of my men and unfortunately in a war sometimes you've got to kill innocent people. I didn't sleep for a week after that because it was the first time I had ever used my pistol."

8.　　Excerpt from Robert De La Rochefoucauld's memoir: *La liberté, C'est mon plaisir.* Paris, 2002.

9.　　Operation Overlord—better known as D-Day—was originally set for 5 June, 1944, but bad weather and heavy seas necessitated a delay until 6 June. Aside from its legendary precursor—the Trojan Horse—the assault of the combined Allied forces on the beaches of Normandy was probably the most successful ruse ever perpetrated against an unsuspecting enemy. The objective was to confuse the German High Command in the hope of convincing its commanders that the long-anticipated invasion of Continental Europe would be aimed at France's northernmost harbour, Pas de Calais, where the distance for crossing The English Channel was the shortest.

In preparation for the expected enemy attack, German forces had been heavily concentrated along the coast well to the north of the true location for the landing. To further emphasize the possibility of a landing at Calais, Allied bombers deliberately carried out a number of raids just prior to the invasion to give the impression that they were 'softening up ' their intended target.

The D-Day landing involved the movement of a total of 3 million men in 47 divisions, moved by 6000 ships with aerial cover provided by 5000 fighter planes. That it was such an overwhelming success (with major casualties only occurring at Juno and Omaha Beach) is indicative of the complex degree of meticulous planning that was required in order to set it in motion.

In the interval, all knowledge of the top-secret machinations necessary for the implementation of the actual D-Day invasion was limited to the inner circle of British and American top brass. Even the leaders of the French, Polish and Dutch and other forces were left in the dark about the exact location of the Allied landing. Such was the extent of the secrecy which was maintained in order to quell any possibility of leaked information falling into the wrong hands! It is said that among those most offended by this exclusion was General de Gaulle in particular, whose relations with both the British and later the Americans had long since become increasingly strained. *The Oxford Companion to World War II.* Oxford: Oxford University Press, 2005.

11. According to Ulrich Herbert, author of *Hitler's Foreign Workers: Enforced Foreign Labour in Germany under the Third Reich* published in 1997 by Cambridge University Press, it was in response to pressure by the German occupying power that the Vichy government established the Service du Travail Obligatoire or compulsory labour service on February 16, 1943. Thereafter all able-bodied young Frenchmen between the ages of 20 and 23 were liable for deportation in order to swell the work force in Nazi Germany by the addition of a new source of foreign workers. Official records reveal that over 700,000 of these less-than-willing young French workers were packed off on freight cars bound for the Third Reich, where they were subjected to the harsh realities of forced labour in the munitions factories, farms, and railways of that increasingly beleaguered nation.

12. Resistance leader, Philippe Vomécourt's account of the period immediately following D-Day includes itemized figures relating to the sabotage operations carried out in June and July of 1944. In all, 600 trains were derailed and 1800 locomotives immobilised along with more than 6000 railway cars. *Who Lived to See the Day: France in Arms, 1940-1945*, p. 218-222.

Chapter 13

1. Excerpt from Robert De La Rochefoucauld's memoir: *La liberté, C'est mon plaisir.* Paris 2002.

2. There seems little doubt that Robert De La Rochefoucauld's mention of Maurice Papon in his memoir reflected his deep personal antipathy towards the instigators of Papon's trial which commenced on 8 October, 1997, after 14 years of turbulent legal wrangling. The trial itself became the longest in French history, finishing on April 2, 1998. During this entire period, l'affaire Papon—as it became known throughout France—was the subject of widespread and sensationalist media coverage.

   In the course of Nazi Germany's Occupation of France, Maurice Papon had served as a high-ranking civil servant in the employ of the collaborationist Vichy Government and had been appointed Secretary-General of the Police in the prefecture of Bordeaux's Gironde district in 1942.

   In 1998—more than fifty years after the fact—Papon was charged and convicted of crimes against humanity for his part in the deportation of more than 1600 Jews to Hitler's death camps. In his defence, Papon testified that he had tried in vain to balance excessive German demands that he dispossess, arrest and finally deport all Jews by declaring that this was against the interests of the honour of France and of the Jews themselves.

Initially, his orders were to round up only foreign Jews, in the hope that at least French Jews would be spared. We must try," Mr. Papon wrote, "to free or, if not free, then at least to keep in the Bordeaux region, Jews worthy of special consideration: holders of the Légion d'Honneur or Croix de Guerre, war invalids, wives of prisoners." But his German masters remained adamant that there should be no exceptions and the fateful deportation orders were reluctantly signed by Secretary-General Papon.

In his defence, it was put forward that in several instances, Papon had been offered and refused promotions—a fact which could be interpreted as an indication of his reluctance to collaborate. A number of prominent political figures and former members of the Resistance—including De La Rochefoucauld—came to his defence, however, in the end, Papon was sentenced to ten years in prison, Due to his advanced age and the continuing controversy over his culpability, his release was secured in 2002.

3.   Excerpt from Robert De La Rochefoucauld's memoir: *La liberté, C'est mon plaisir*. Paris, 2002.

Chapter 14

1.   Edgard de Larminat (November 1895—1962) was a highly-decorated French general, who served in both World I and World War II. He was one of the most important military figures to align himself with the Free French forces in 1940 and saw active service in North Africa before participating in the liberation of both Italy and France.

2.   François VI, Duc De La Rochefoucauld (1613 –1680) remains among France's most celebrated authors, largely due to the brilliance of his book of 503 maxims first published in 1665. These maxims have since been widely translated and it has long been acknowledged that his pithy words of wisdom are indisputably representative of a wealth of universal truths concerning the human condition. *Encyclopædia Britannica* (11th ed.). Cambridge University Press.

3.   Excerpt from Robert De La Rochefoucauld's memoir: *La liberté, C'est mon plaisir*. Paris, 2002.

4.   Ibid.

5.   Ibid.

6.   Ibid

7. Ten months after D-Day, an Allied operation against the German forces defending Royan and the Pointe de Grave area at the mouth of the Gironde began with a general naval bombardment on April 15, 1945, For five days, an American naval task force in conjunction with an aerial assault assisted the Free French ground forces. American B-17 Flying Fortress and B-24 Liberator aircraft carried out bombing missions, which purportedly involved the pioneering use of napalm. More than 3,000 French civilians had not yet evacuated the town of Royan and half their number were either killed or injured as a result of these devastating air raids.

8. On May 7, 1945, Germany signed an unconditional surrender at Allied headquarters in Reims, France to take effect the following day, and bring official closure to the conflict in the European theatre of World War II. This was reported in an Associated Press story under the headline "The War in Europe is Ended!"

    "The Germans were asked sternly if they understand the surrender terms imposed upon Germany and if they would be carried out by Germany. They answered 'Yes'. Germany, which began the war with a ruthless attack upon Poland, followed by successive aggressions and brutality in internment camps, surrendered with an appeal to the victors for mercy toward the German people and its armed forces." *The New York Times.*

Chapter 15
Aftermath

1. General Roger-Jean-Charles-Jean Noiret (1895-1976) served his country with distinction in post-war Germany and was appointed as Commander-in-Chief of French Forces there from 1951-1956.

2. Marshall Georgy Konstantinovich Zhukov (1896-1974) the most decorated general in the history of the Soviet Union served as a career officer in the Red Army and played a crucial role in the defence of his homeland in the wake of the Nazi invasion of Russia in July 1941. Under his leadership, Soviet troops eventually thrust through much of Eastern Europe to effect the liberation of the Soviet Union and other occupied nations. In the Spring of 1945, he advanced relentlessly to seize control of Berlin, and, in the wake of the German surrender, was appointed by Stalin as Commander-in-chief of the Soviet Occupying Power.

    Zhukov has been widely regarded as the most outstanding general of World War II, largely due to the number and scale of victories amassed under his leadership. Both Britain's General Bernard Montgomery and Supreme Allied

Commander in Europe, General Dwight D. Eisenhower, recognized and respected Zhukov's extraordinary capacity for inspiring his troops in conjunction with his unique genius for strategy, often against overwhelming odds. Harold Shukman, *Stalin's Generals*, Grove Press, New York City, (1993).

3.   Excerpt from Robert De La Rochefoucauld's memoir: *La liberté, C'est mon plaisir.* Paris, 2002.

Epilogue

1.   This fraternity of former parachutist secret agents originating from France, Britain and Belgium was formed in 1945 and thereafter the group banded together for an annual reunion in one or other of the three countries. By coincidence, it was during a reunion held in France at the family home, Villeneuve, that one of these former operatives chanced to meet and subsequently marry one of De La Rochefoucauld's younger sisters.

2.   During World War II, Philippe de Hauteclocque joined De Gaulle's Free French forces after the fall of France and made his way to London. Here he adopted the pseudonym "Jacques-Philippe Leclerc" and went on to serve with distinction in Tunisia.

After D-Day, General Leclerc's 2nd Armoured Division took part in the battle of the Falaise Pocket before proceeding to Paris to liberate the city on 16 August,1944. At the end of hostilities in Europe, he was placed in command of the French Far East Expeditionary Corps *(Corps expéditionnaire français en Extrême-Orient,* CEFEO) and represented France at the official surrender of Japan in September 1945.

In his capacity as the commander-in-chief, Leclerc was posted to French Indochina, first cracking a Viet Minh blockade around Saigon, then driving through the Mekong delta and north into the highlands.

In November 1947, General Jacques-Philippe Leclerc de Hauteclocque died tragically as the result of a plane crash in French Algeria, and was posthumously awarded the title of Marshal of France in 1952.

3.   Following the re-occupation of Indochina by the French in 1945 in the wake of the Japanese surrender, Viet Minh rebels in the north launched a campaign against the governing authority in the colonies of French Indochina. At the outset, the conflict was confined to low-level rural insurgency, however, after Chinese communist troops reached the Northern border of Vietnam in 1949, the controversial struggle evolved into a conventional war. In France, among its detractors, it became known as the "dirty war" *(la sale guerre)* and culminated in a decisive French defeat at the Battle of Dien Bien Phu in 1954.

INDEX

ABOUT THE AUTHOR

Carolyn Gossage was born in Toronto and as an only child, the allure of books and writing claimed her as an early victim. After studying French and German, at the University of Toronto's University College, she spent a year at the Sorbonne in Paris, before returning to Toronto to teach at the University of Toronto's Lab School—The Institute of Child Study English and subsequently at Canada's National Ballet School, publishing her first book in 1977.

CAROLYN GOSSAGE
AUTHOR PHOTO
Photo by Elisabetta Rossi.

While continuing to write, she began working in the film industry on features and series including *Road to Avonlea* and *Goosebumps*. Carolyn Gossage also became the collaborative author of a major art history publication, *Ethiopian Icons* published by Skira in Milan. Her extensive travels in Ethiopia led to *Ethiopian Crosses* and most recently she collaborated on *Basilicas of Ethiopia—An Architectural History*.

She is also passionate about The Great Outdoors which includes bass fishing and cross-country-skiing at every opportunity.